D1604813

CHINESE MYTHOLOGY ROCKS!

Titles in the Mythology Rocks! Series

African Mythology Rocks!
ISBN: 978-0-7660-3896-7
Paperback Ed. 978-1-59845-328-7

Celtic Mythology Rocks!
ISBN: 978-0-7660-3895-0
Paperback Ed. 978-1-59845-326-3

Chinese Mythology Rocks!
ISBN: 978-0-7660-3898-1
Paperback Ed. 978-1-59845-330-0

Gods and Goddesses in Greek Mythology Rocks!
ISBN: 978-0-7660-3897-4
Paperback Ed. 978-1-59845-329-4

Heroes in Greek Mythology Rocks!
ISBN: 978-0-7660-3900-1
Paperback Ed. 978-1-59845-331-7

Maya & Aztec Mythology Rocks!
ISBN: 978-0-7660-3899-8
Paperback Ed. 978-1-59845-327-0

Mythology Rocks!

CHINESE MYTHOLOGY ROCKS!

Irene Dea Collier

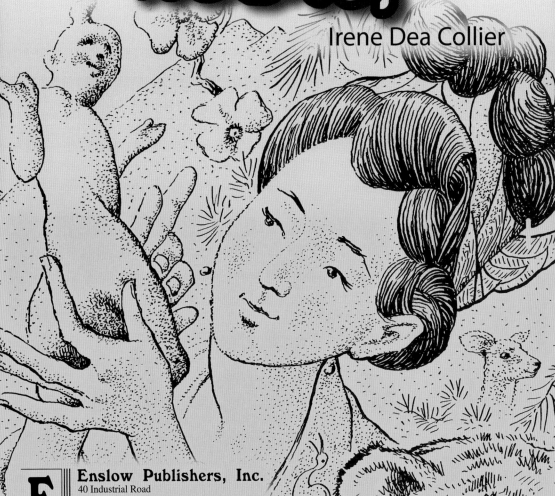

Enslow Publishers, Inc.
40 Industrial Road
Box 398
Berkeley Heights, NJ 07922
USA

http://www.enslow.com

For Malcolm, Alina, Lora, and Aram.

Original edition published as *Chinese Mythology* in 2001

Library of Congress Cataloging-in-Publication Data

Collier, Irene Dea.
    Chinese Mythology Rocks / Irene Dea Collier.
        p. cm. — (Mythology rocks!)
    Includes bibliographical references and index.
    Summary: "Read how Panku created the world and Nuwa created people, the grand archer Yi, and seven other important Chinese myths"—Provided by publisher.
    ISBN: 978-0-7660-3898-1
    1. Mythology, Chinese—Juvenile literature. I. Title.
    BL1825.C64 2012
    398.20951—dc22
    2010053391

Paperback ISBN: 978-1-59845-330-0

Printed in China

052011 Leo Paper Group, Heshan City, Guangdong, China.

10 9 8 7 6 5 4 3 2 1

To Our Readers: We have done our best to make sure all Internet addresses in this book were active and appropriate when we went to press. However, the author and the publisher have no control over and assume no liability for the material available on those Internet sites or on other Web sites they may link to. Any comments or suggestions can be sent by e-mail to comments@enslow.com or to the address on the back cover.

Cover and illustrations by William Sauts Bock

Contents

Preface

The Chinese heaven is filled with many images: mythical rulers, religious gods and goddesses, historical beings, writers, poets, philosophers, dragons, phoenixes, tortoises, unicorns, rare birds, and flowering fruit trees. Figures from conflicting time periods, different religions, and opposing philosophies appear and interact in Chinese myths. In many Chinese tales, there is no clear separation between the mythical and the real, between heaven and earth, between history and early storytelling, between past and present.

> China is a mosaic of diverse groups and of multitudes of traditions.
> . . . When we speak of Chinese mythology we need to be clear that
> it represents streams flowing together, running parallel, merging
> or diverging from many places and from many different models of
> reality.[1]

Myths contain strong influences from Chinese folk religion, Confucianism, Taoism, and Buddhism. Chinese folk religion, the oldest of the four, pays homage to ancestors who watch from afar and guide the lives of those still living on earth. In the fifth century B.C., the philosopher Confucius introduced his ideas, which stressed fulfilling obligations and maintaining proper conduct. Although Confucianism is not a religion, its influence is deeply ingrained in Chinese ideas about behavior and government.

Between 600–300 B.C. Taoism emerged. At first, it was a philosophy that encouraged people to seek harmony with the Tao, or the Way, a nature force. Later, it evolved into a religious system involving many gods, goddesses, spirits, ghosts, demons, magical powers, and the quest for immortality.

In A.D. 67 Buddhism was introduced to China from India. It contributed two powerful religious and mythical figures: the Buddha, a real, historical person who later became a divinity, and Kuan Yin, the goddess of mercy. It also introduced the concept of reincarnation, the idea that a person may be reborn into another life.

Myths might contain elements and characters from all of these sources, and for this book we have chosen stories that reflect their influences.

Many of the ancient myths are from the fabled era of the "Ten Legendary Kings," a time before the dawn of history. Thereafter, the historical period of Chinese history is divided into a series of dynasties until the year 1911, the beginning of the period of modern government. A dynasty is a succession of rulers, all from the same family. Each dynasty was unique in its approach and accomplishments. Since each ruling family came into power in a period of upheaval, the dates of each dynasty are only approximate, and are strongly debated by Chinese scholars old and new. The major dynasties and their dates are listed on page 12.

In addition to the diversity of opinion regarding dates in Chinese history, there are many systems for spelling the names of the Chinese dynasties and other Chinese words. In the interest of making this text easy for students of all nationalities to follow, we have attempted to use the easiest pronunciation for dynasties, names, and places.

In some cases, we have kept the traditional and familiar transliterations of Chinese words that appear in older books. In other cases, we have used the *pinyin* system, which has been promoted by the Chinese government since the 1970s. At that time, the government wanted to standardize all foreign language translations using the Mandarin dialect of Chinese. In

Ten Legendary Kings[2]

After the Chinese settled in the Yangtze Valley in 6500 B.C.
After the Chinese settled in the Yellw River Valley in 5000 B.C.

Early Chinese stories refer to a mythical time ruled by the Ten Legendary Kings. These rulers are half-human, half-animal. They have magical powers and introduce knowledge to humans such as writing, agriculture, hunting, fire, and flood control. Although no archaeological evidence exists to prove they really lived, these kings dominated early Chinese mythology.

Name:	Dates:	Known for:
Fushi	3000 B.C	fire, hunting, trigrams, domestication of animals
Shen Nung	2737–2598 B.C.	agriculture, medicine
Yen Di	brief rule	overthrown by his brother, Huang Di
Huang Di (Yellow Emperor)	2697–2598 B.C.	dams, compass, calendar, coins
Shao Hao	2598–2591 B.C.	few accomplishments
Kao Yang	indeterminate time	father of eight famous sons
K'u	indeterminate time	uncertain accomplishments
Yao Ti (Divine Yao)	2357–2255 B.C.	astronomy, canal building
Shun	2317–2208 B.C.	dams
Yu the Great	2205–2197 B.C.	mapping, flood control, founder of the legendary Xia Dynasty, 2005–1520 B.C., which has not yet been verified.

Major Historical Dynasties[3]

Name:	Dates:	Known for:
Shang	1523–1027 B.C.	High Bronze Age
Zhou [Joh]	1027–221 B.C.	feudalism, Confucius, great classics
Qin [Chin]	221–206 B.C.	burning of books, Great Wall, bureaucracy, standardized measures
Han	206 B.C.–A.D. 220	trade along the Silk Road, art, science
Six Dynasties	220–589	disunity, Buddhism firmly established
Sui	590–617	Great Canal
Tang	618–906	Golden Age, literature, art
Song	960–1279	landscape painting
Yuan	1280–1367	Mongol Dynasty: Genghis Khan
Ming	1368–1643	porcelain, public works
Qing [Ching]	1644–1911	Manchu Dynasty: disintegration

period of modern government	1911 1949	establishment of the republic establishment of the People's Republic of China

pinyin, the letter q is pronounced "*ch*," the letter x is pronounced "*sh*," and the letters zh are pronounced "*j*." Students who wish to pursue further research, either in books or online, should be aware of the special, varied nature of Chinese transliterations. Who would think, for example, that Hsi Wang Mu and Xiwangmu are one and the same? Or that Kong Fuzi is the same as Confucius? Since any particular transliteration system can go in and out of vogue, it is important to be aware that many possible spellings exist for Chinese words.

Another difficulty is trying to separate Chinese myth and Chinese history. Before the invention of writing, myths had been passed down through the oral tradition for thousands of years. Many of these stories were originally based on actual historical events and people; however, mythical elements were soon interwoven into the tales. Like many other groups of people, the Chinese used myths to explain their history.

To make the task of separating myth from history even more difficult, many history books were burned in 213 B.C. by Qinshihuangdi [Chin shi wong dee], the emperor of the Qin [Chin] dynasty. In order to proclaim himself the first emperor of China, he ordered a massive burning of books concerning history, literature, and music. A hundred years later, Confucian scholars attempted to reconstruct China's history from bits and pieces of the few surviving texts. These scholars did not hesitate to change existing myths or to discard information to suit their own philosophy.

Myths were rarely considered worthy of scholarly attention and consisted of a few sketchy lines in the Chinese classical literature that managed to survive. Despite their limited appeal to scholars, myths were kept alive by strong oral and artistic traditions. Myths were freely adapted and passed along by storytellers, merchants, travelers, muralists, sculptors, painters, Chinese opera and theater troupes, puppeteers, and novelists.

In the 1920s, the Chinese government finally attempted to collect myths told by the peasants. Scholars were astounded by the volume and variety of the stories they found. By then, each province had developed its own beloved version, or several versions, of the ancient stories. There was little consistency found in the mythology. Unlike the Greeks, whose pantheon, or collection of gods and heroes, is well defined and frozen in time with the passing of their civilization, the Chinese are still changing and evolving their mythology, just as their country's history also continues to evolve. Today, television producers, moviemakers, animation artists, and computer game designers carry out the tradition of reinventing ancient myths to fit modern times.

Despite having many themes and variations throughout the centuries, most Chinese myths contain one common central element: the survival of ordinary people against great odds, sometimes aided by the gods, sometimes punished or inhibited by them. The quest for food and shelter is an essential one, facing Chinese people even today, as overpopulation and natural disasters continue to strike. Individual acts of self-sacrifice and initiative are still essential to solve problems faced by the common man. Now, as in the past, at the core of many myths is the story of the people's struggle to survive on this beautiful, fragile, and unsteady planet.

1

Panku Creates the World

INTRODUCTION

The earliest Chinese texts contain many myths about wondrous rulers of ancient times; however, there are no creation stories to be found among them. The story of Panku is probably the closest Chinese version of a creation myth. It first appears in the Han dynasty (206 B.C.–A.D. 220), hundreds of years after the first stories were told about the ancient rulers.

Many experts believe that the story of Panku was molded and influenced by the caravan traders who wound across the deserts and mountains of the Middle East, India, Africa, and China carrying silk, spices, and other precious items of trade.[1] The Panku story shares some common elements with creation myths of those far-flung regions: a cosmic egg, separation of the world into opposing forces, and doomed gods.

This story introduces the important concept of *yin* and *yang*. These opposing forces, which exist in everything found in nature, are not seen as evil and good, but as dark and light, female and male, earth and heaven. One cannot exist without the other.

In this story, Panku is depicted as a giant. In other versions, he appears in his withered human form, clothed in bearskin and leaves.

Panku Creates the World

Once, the world was a mass of swirling darkness. There was no heaven. There was no earth. All the forces of the universe were trapped inside a small egg, tumbling and spinning in utter chaos.

Inside the egg was a tiny creature named Panku. He slept soundly, unbothered by the disorder around him. As he slept, Panku grew, and the egg also grew around him. For eighteen thousand years Panku slumbered peacefully, until he had developed into a well-formed, muscular giant whose body spanned ninety thousand *li* (about thirty thousand miles). In perfect harmony with Panku's body, the eggshell also stretched, straining to hold both the expanding giant and the turbulent gases of the world inside its boundaries.

One day when the universe was especially unstable, Panku woke up. All around, he saw nothing but darkness and confusion. At first, he was intrigued by the irregular rhythms of the world. He watched, fascinated, as whirling particles burst and scattered around him. Quickly, he learned to dodge exploding gases by nimbly jumping from side to side.

After awhile, however, he became tired of all the noise and confusion. The constant commotion jangled his nerves. The din produced a ringing in his ears that made him extremely irritable. The longer he watched the chaos of the universe, the more he longed for the tranquility of his deep sleep. The chaos bothered him, but even more important, Panku realized that the fragile shell of the universe might rupture at any moment.

Panku knew he would have to take action, so he waited until the world was in a state of uneasy calm, then grabbed a long meteor. He picked it up like an ax and swung it down with every ounce of his strength. It crashed upon the exact center of the egg with a huge sonic boom. The sound reverberated throughout the world and split all the particles and gases of the universe in two. The light, pure forces of the world drifted up and formed the blue heavens. The heavy, dark forces of the universe sank down and formed the fertile earth.

Panku was delighted with his new world. It had beauty, order, and peace. To preserve these conditions, he propped up the sky with his strong arms, wedging his body between heaven and earth. Each day, the sky rose ten *li* as Panku stretched and shoved it higher and higher.

For eons, he held up the sky without complaint, determined that the world should not dissolve back into chaos. As time passed, however, he became weary as his cramped muscles tightened from the weight of the world. For centuries, Panku pushed in agony with every sinew, muscle, and bone of his body. He cried out for help, but his voice just echoed in the emptiness. No other living creature was around to hear him. Each day he longed for relief; each day he received none. He struggled for tens of thousands of years until heaven and earth each lost its memory of the other—and were forever separated into the forces of *yin*, the dark, and *yang*, the light.

When the sky was firmly attached to the heavens and the earth was soundly anchored below, Panku finally lost his resolve. Slowly, he grew weaker and older. His body gradually shrank and wrinkled. His muscles loosened, and his breath

became faint. After centuries of stretching and straining, the reliable giant fell to the ground, exhausted and drained.

His massive, withered body covered the earth gently like a carpet. His flesh crumbled and spread rich, dark nutrients and sweet smelling soil upon the barren ground. His beads of sweat sprinkled droplets of rain and dew on the soft fertile earth. The tangled hair on his head and beard became the stiff branches of trees and bushes. The hair on his arms turned into tiny leaves, trailing vines, and delicate flowers. His teeth and bones broke into bits of shiny metals—gold, silver, and copper—which embedded themselves deep in the earth. His bone marrow hardened into creamy, translucent jade in colors of lavender, green, and white. His blood trickled over the land to create large pools and swift rivers. His voice, even in its weakness, produced rolling thunder and crackling lightning. His dying breath formed blowing winds and puffy clouds. Finally, released from his suffering, Panku sobbed tears of gratitude which fell and created glittering, vast bodies of water that became the oceans.

Finally his work was over, and Panku, the creator, was dead. In his place, he left a world that sparkled and twinkled with splashes of bright blues, vibrant greens, dusky browns, and clear, cold rushing waters.

QUESTIONS AND ANSWERS

Q: *Why was an egg a good symbol for the beginning of the world?*

A: Many creatures are born from eggs, a symbol of life. Each egg is round like the world, and contains all the nutrients essential for developing life.

Q: *What were Panku's first feelings about chaos, and how did they change?*

A: Initially, he was fascinated by the noise and exploding gases, but later the noise and disorder irritated him, and he longed to return to his peaceful sleeping state.

Q: *Why did Panku continue to hold up the world?*

A: He wanted the world to be orderly and quiet. He did not want the world to destroy itself and return to the chaos that existed before.

Q: *How were the forces of the world divided?*

A: The light, pure forces called the *yang* drifted into heaven; the heavy, dark forces called the *yin* sank down to earth.

Q: *Was Panku happy when he died?*

A: Yes, even when people have a difficult life, they can be happy at the end of that life if they have accomplished something worthwhile.

EXPERT COMMENTARY

In his comparison of world mythologies, anthropologist Roy Willis writes about the death of Panku:

> In many traditions, creation is brought about by sacrificial death. . . . This story [of Panku] resembles a Vedic hymn of the Indian tradition which tells how Purusha, a primordial being, is sacrificed: his bodily parts then become the many components of the universe, including gods, man and animals. In Saharan Africa the world was originally made out of the numerous segments of the sacrificed cosmic serpent Minia, God's first creation–an event remembered in animal sacrifice in the region to this day. There is a similar cosmic drama in an Assyro—Babylonian myth when the celestial king Marduk slaughters the serpent Tiamat, the feminine principle of chaos, and divides her enormous corpse: from one half Marduk constructs the vault of heaven, from the other the solid earth. . . .[2]

The story of Panku also introduces one of the most important concepts in Chinese thought: *yin* and *yang*. Authors Martin Palmer and Zhao Xiaomin of the International Consultancy on Religion, Education, and Culture (ICOREC) explain:

> Yin is female, moist, cold, the moon, the autumn and winter, the shadow and the waters. Yang is male, dry, hot, the sun, the spring and summer, the bright and the dry land. They struggle with each other for supremacy. From their struggle comes the dynamic which drives the whole of life. For they are found locked together in every being, every situation. As one seems to be gaining the ascendancy, the other arises for they each carry the seed of the other within them as the yin yang symbol so clearly illustrates.[3]

2

Nuwa Creates People

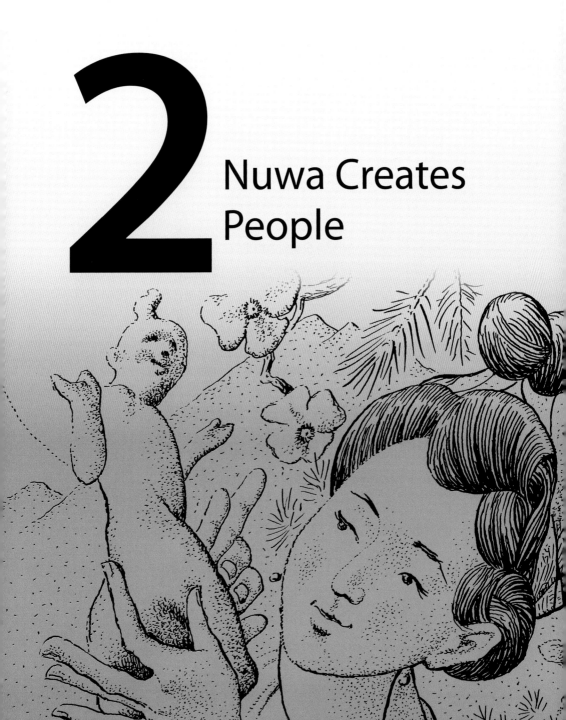

INTRODUCTION

Whereas Panku, the creator of the universe was male, the creator of people was a female goddess named Nuwa. Nuwa is briefly mentioned in several ancient Chinese texts, *A Classic of History* (eighth century B.C.), *A Classic of Mountains and Seas* (third century B.C.), and *Questions of Heaven* (fourth century B.C.).[1]

In addition, many images of Nuwa have been uncovered on ancient Chinese bronze sculptures and paintings. Like many of the early Chinese gods, Nuwa was half animal, half divine. Most often, Nuwa had the face and arms of a human but the body of a snake or dragon. She could change her shape at will. Modern Chinese books prefer to show her as a beautiful woman.

It appeared that women in China had no social standing of their own. However, in their roles as mothers and wives, they were extremely powerful. Since women generally outlived their husbands, they often asserted themselves and ran the household after their spouses' death. Even in politics, several women (empresses) became extremely powerful after the death of their husbands, the emperors.[2]

Although most gods were male, Nuwa is a very powerful female goddess in early mythology. She creates mankind and is responsible for repairing the earth.

Nuwa Creates People

The world was indeed a sparkling jewel. Sturdy pine trees dotted the mountains, and weeping willows lined the streams. Apple, quince, and plum blossoms burst into bloom and later yielded ripe, heavy fruit. Birds flitted about in the azure sky, leaving their black, crimson, and iridescent green feathers drifting in the wind. Silverfish and carp splashed gleefully in the waterways. Fierce beasts like tigers and gentle creatures like deer roamed with equal abandon across the rocky hills.

Nuwa, a goddess, stumbled accidentally upon this vibrant world during her travels. The earth was humming and teeming with life. She marveled at its many wondrous creatures. Everywhere she looked, she found a creature more marvelous than the one before. She saw every type of fur and fin, feather and scale, horn, hoof, and stinger. Creatures lumbered, crawled, and slithered upon the earth. They jumped, darted, and roiled in the sea. Scented flowers like jasmine, hyacinth, and narcissus wrapped the entire world in their warm, strong perfume.

But as she explored its niches and crannies, Nuwa began to feel strangely dissatisfied with the budding world. The goddess found it to be enchanting, but empty. It felt lonely to Nuwa, who sat by a river to ponder her feelings. She gazed at her reflection in the water, and suddenly she knew what was missing: She wanted the world to be filled with thinking, laughing creatures like herself.

The river stretched out before her, its waves slapping the shore. The cloudy green waters left a rim of thick yellow earth along its banks. Nuwa felt its slippery texture with her fingertips and scooped out a ball of clay. The cool, sticky earth deposited by the river was perfect for her task, and she rolled the damp clay into a doll, giving it a head, shoulders, chest, and arms like her own. For the doll's lower body, she hesitated. Nuwa considered giving it scales and claws like a lizard, or fins and tails like a fish. Both shapes were quite useful, since the goddess frequently changed the shape of her own lower body to be able to get around the oceans and the heavens quickly. Finally, she decided to attach legs to the new creature so it could both walk on land and paddle about in the sea.

From the many shades of yellow earth, Nuwa made tall dolls and short dolls. She made thin dolls and fat dolls. She made curly-haired dolls and straight-haired dolls. She made dolls with eyes as round and large as cherries, some with eyes as long and narrow as a mosquito's wing. She made some with eyes so dark they looked like the midnight sky, others so light they looked like liquid honey. Each creature was different, so the goddess could recognize her creations. Then, as she breathed on each doll, it sprang to life, giggling and hopping about.

Nuwa was so delighted with her handiwork that she wanted to make more. But she needed a quicker method. Along the riverbanks, slender reeds arched their graceful stems over the water. Nuwa rolled up her sleeves, cut a reed, and dipped it into the river mud like a spoon. Expertly, she flicked her wrist and dropped blobs of mud on the ground. When they dried, she breathed a huge puff of air into each blob, and instantly they became round, smiling creatures. The cheerful laughter of her creatures filled the goddess with happiness and pride.

However, Nuwa was tired. As much as she loved her new creations, she knew she could not watch over these humans every second. What would happen to these creatures when they grew old and died? Nuwa did not relish making repairs, nor did she wish to repeat the tiring task of making new people. She thought and thought. How could these creatures reproduce without her?

With a twist and a poke, she made some of the clay creatures male and some of them female. Then she gathered up all the noisy creatures who were slipping and falling in the mud. In the hubbub, she began to deliver her most important instructions. As Nuwa spoke, the clamor died down to a silent hush. The humans listened solemnly to her words. She spoke of the importance of marriage and a couple's obligations to each other. She told them how to make children and how to raise them. She wished them a long and joyful existence on their earth. As the goddess left, she expressed her fervent hope that they would make new people and live happily without her. Then she ascended to the sky seated in a thundering chariot pulled by six winged dragons.

To this day, people continue to marry and have children who brighten the world with their joyous laughter, just as the dancing mud dolls did in the days of Nuwa.

QUESTIONS AND ANSWERS

Q: *Why was Nuwa dissatisfied with the beautiful world?*

A: The world felt empty, and she wanted to populate it with creatures like herself, who could think, talk, and laugh.

Q: *What are the two ways that Nuwa created human beings?*

A: She took river mud and shaped the first people by hand. Later, she dipped a reed into the mud and flicked blobs of mud onto the ground. When she breathed on the mud creatures, they sprang to life.

Q: *Why was it important to the goddess to make each mud doll different?*

A: Nuwa wanted to be able to recognize each of her creations. It was satisfying to make each one different, and the process of creation made her very happy.

Q: *Why did she want her creations to make their own children?*

A: She did not want to stay on earth to watch over them, nor did she want to return to earth to make or repair humans. She wanted the humans to learn to live on their own without the help of the gods.

Q: *What feelings do people share with the gods of old in the creation process?*

A: People are delighted and proud of each new creation, or child, who brings joy and laughter to the world.

EXPERT COMMENTARY

Jan and Yvonne Walls are two noted sinologists, or scholars who study Chinese language and culture. They point out that Chinese gods have four basic types of physical forms:

> Of the four characteristic form-types—human form, beast form, half-human-half-beast form, and composite form of several animals—those of a purely human form are in a definite minority in the classical [Chinese] pantheon. Almost all the gods are, in fact, represented as half-human, half-beast. . . . It is only in later centuries, with the introduction of Buddhist and Taoist pantheons that most primary gods and goddesses are totally human in appearance.[3]

Professor Anne Birrell of the University of Cambridge finds similarities in the creation of people in other cultures:

> Most etiological [origin] myths of the creation of humankind narrate that the substance from which humans were made was dust, as in *Genesis* [part of the Bible], or else earth, or dirt or clay. . . . In this myth of Nü Kua [Nuwa], humans are made from the materials of yellow earth and mud.[4]

Professor Birrell adds:

> A second worldwide motif is that of social stratification. In the Nü Kua [Nuwa] myth humans are polarized into "rich aristocrats" made from yellow earth and "poor commoners" made from mud.[5]

3 Fushi Teaches the People

INTRODUCTION

The earliest myths involve the Ten Legendary Kings (see page 11), gods who guided people through their prehistoric beginnings (roughly 3000–2197 B.C.).[1] These early rulers were demigods, or half god and half human, who lived among the people and taught them the rules of civilization. They could change into the shapes of animals or remain in their half-god, half-animal state. Eventually, they retired to the heavens when their time on earth expired.

Fushi was the first ruler of this magical period. Many scholars believe that his story is based on an actual monarch who lived sometime between 2953–2736 B.C.[2] However, whether he was based on a real person or not, Fushi is a beloved figure in mythology who taught survival skills to early humans. These include using fire, fishing, hunting, writing, and fortune-telling. In some stories, Fushi is described as having the body of a human. In other stories, he has the head of a human and the body of a snake. In many stories he is the husband of Nuwa, and together they are the bearers of civilization.

In the story, Fushi introduces the trigrams, which are patterns made with short and long sticks. People threw down six sticks and then interpreted the patterns they formed. In the beginning, the interpretations of the trigrams were passed down orally, then were finally written down centuries later between 1059–249 B.C. Today, the collected trigrams are known as the *I Ching* [ee jihng], or *The Book of Changes*. Even in ancient times, this book was considered so important that it was one of the few Chinese texts spared in the book burning of 213 B.C. Many people still read this book to uncover its philosophy, as well as to benefit from its prophecies.

In mythology, Fushi is credited with introducing writing, which was was invented to improve upon the ancient tally system of tying knots. However, its creation has also been attributed to T'sang Chieh, a palace record keeper who lived around 2500 B.C.[3] Some of the earliest Chinese writing consisted of simple lines and picture symbols that could be scratched easily onto stones, turtle shells, and animal bones. By 1600 B.C., the writing system was quite advanced; its symbols are found on numerous bronze vessels from that period. During the Qin dynasty (221–206 B.C.), Chinese writing became systematized and sophisticated. Many of the symbols from that era closely resemble the Chinese writing characters used today.[4]

Fushi Teaches the People

Fushi watched the new humans stumbling about. These people did not have the supernatural powers of gods, the strength of tigers, or the speed of leopards. They did not have the protective armor of turtles, the leathery hide of water buffaloes, or the thick fur of foxes. People had thin skin, soft flesh, sparse hair, and moved about rather slowly. They had good hearts and cheerful laughter, but they were easily frightened and discouraged. Fushi decided to help the new humans.

First, Fushi taught people how to twist plant fibers together to form ropes of all widths and lengths. With the thinner ropes, he wove fishing lines and nets so people could plunge the water's depths to find food. With the thicker ropes, he braided strong bridges, then strung them across high chasms so people could cross from one mountain peak to another in search of food.

When lightning set trees on fire, as so often happened, the people trembled and hid in caves. To entice the people to come out, Fushi twirled together two willow sticks to start a fire. He showed the humans how cooked meat and fish were more digestible and tempting than raw meat and fish. The people soon discovered that fire could also keep them safe and snug throughout the chilly nights. Ferocious animals feared its licking flames, and biting insects avoided its sooty smoke.

In the spring, Fushi shaped young branches over an open fire, then cooled them into curvy bows. He scraped, smoothed, and dried slender sticks into arrow shafts. Then Fushi led the people on hunts for deer, wild boar, and migrant birds. He guided them in gathering up black mushrooms of the forests, wild grasses of the plains, and bitter cresses growing along the banks of trickling streams. He taught them how to raise sheep, goats, geese, and ducks. Fushi warned people only to take what they needed and never to waste food or kill senselessly.

To keep track of the food they grew and exchanged, people tied fancy knots shaped like butterflies, flowers, and diamonds. But they often forgot what each knot meant and argued and fought among themselves, so Fushi invented a writing system by scratching small pictures and numbers onto shells and bones. Each picture stood for a word. People copied the curving shapes of words onto turtle shells, bamboo sticks, and animal bones to remind themselves of their debts.

Fushi knew that he could not stay on earth forever to help the people make up their minds whenever they were in trouble. When they did not know which path to take or which way to turn, Fushi taught them how to consult the oracle. First, he took a turtle's shell and copied its eight-sided edges in the dirt. Then, on each edge, he drew three lines, or a trigram.

On the edge, Fushi drew three straight lines to represent heaven:

——
——
——

On the opposite edge, he drew three broken lines to represent earth:

— —
— —
— —

Water had one solid middle line between two broken lines; fire, its opposite, had one broken middle line between two solid lines.

$$
\begin{array}{cc}
\text{— —} & \text{———} \\
\text{———} & \text{— —} \\
\text{— —} & \text{———}
\end{array}
$$

A broken line below two solid lines signaled wind and wood; one solid line below two broken lines signaled storm and thunder.

$$
\begin{array}{cc}
\text{———} & \text{— —} \\
\text{———} & \text{— —} \\
\text{— —} & \text{———}
\end{array}
$$

Two broken strokes below a solid line showed mountain; two solid strokes below a broken line showed lake.

$$
\begin{array}{cc}
\text{———} & \text{— —} \\
\text{— —} & \text{———} \\
\text{— —} & \text{———}
\end{array}
$$

Then Fushi showed people how to use these trigrams. He found a yarrow plant and pulled off its feathery leaves and tiny yellow flowers, so that only the straight stalks remained. He broke the straight stalks into short pieces and long pieces. He mixed them up and threw pieces on the ground six times, arranging them in rows. The short pieces stood for broken lines; the long pieces stood for solid lines. Fushi taught people how to interpret the meaning of the sticks.

He gathered up the stalks and threw down new stalks of yarrow again and again. No matter what pattern of short and long sticks appeared, they always resembled two trigrams, such as earth/water, wind/fire, thunder/lake. Each time, Fushi taught people the meaning of the patterns. Some patterns might mean the people were safe; others might warn them of impending danger. Some patterns advised them to stay in place; others advised them to move. Some urged them to attack, and some urged them to yield in battle. By reading the

patterns of the sticks, the people could unlock their fortunes and make choices about their actions.

The people were delighted with their knowledge and felt ready to populate the earth. But Fushi knew better. He realized that finding food, making tools, raising animals, keeping records, and making choices were not enough.

He worried that the people would become boastful and selfish. Fushi wanted them to stay humble and learn from their past, to remember their successes and failures by telling stories. To help the storytellers, and to touch their hearts, he gave them his last gift, the gift of music.

Fushi taught the people how to make a Chinese lute, a *pípa*. Its melodic notes were a pleasure to hear, and its beautiful curves were a joy to behold. The *pípa* could mimic the sound of wind blowing against trees, water flowing over rocks, and horses' hooves clopping forward in battle. Fushi taught the people how to use the *pípa* to tell unforgettable stories.

Each time the people plucked a tune, the still air in the sound box of the *pípa* sprang to life. Each time they strummed the strings, sleeping emotions and silent thoughts welled up in their hearts and minds. Playing the *pípa* filled the people's bodies with joy, calmed their most savage feelings, and eased their deepest sorrows.

When his time on earth was over, Fushi bade goodbye to his people and ascended to the heavens, hoping that they would share their wisdom with each other and continue to live in peace.

QUESTIONS AND ANSWERS

Q: *What did Fushi teach people about fire?*

A: They could use it for cooking, warmth, and keeping away animals and insects.

Q: *What types of food did Fushi teach people to gather or hunt for?*

A: He taught them how to gather wild plants, such as mushrooms, cresses, and wild grasses. And he taught them how to catch fish, raise animals, and hunt for deer, wild boar, and birds.

Q: *What warnings did Fushi give to his people, and what qualities did these warnings try to discourage in humans?*

A: He warned people never to waste food or to be greedy and take more food than they needed.

Q: *What systems did Fushi invent to keep track of the amounts of food the people grew and traded?*

A: First Fushi taught the people to tie knots. When this system failed to work, Fushi invented a pictogram system of writing.

Q: *Why did people want to foretell the future?*

A: They were unsure of themselves and could not make up their minds. They needed some way to make decisions when Fushi and the other gods would no longer be around.

Q: *What is the collected book of trigrams called?*

A: It is called the *I Ching* or *The Book of Changes*.

Q: *Why did Fushi think that storytelling was important to the people?*

A: Hearing stories, people could learn from the mistakes of the past and remain humble.

Q: *How was the gift of music different from the gifts of fire, food, and weapons?*

A: The gift of music spoke to a person's soul and emotional well-being. Music went beyond the basic needs for survival, such as food, fire, and shelter. It uplifted the people's spirit and encouraged them to keep a "literary" history or oral tradition.

EXPERT COMMENTARY

The tortoise and yarrow have symbolic meaning in the story. In his work on cyclic world myths, professor Robert Shanmu Chen of the University of British Columbia writes:

> Divination of the Pa Kua [eight-sided octagon] was accomplished through the use of the tortoise-shell and the arrangement of stalks of milfoil [also known as yarrow]. The tortoise was the sacred animal of the north-winter, a hibernal animal capable of seemingly occult death and rebirth, while the milfoil was regarded as a sacred plant bearing three hundred stems every thousand years and connected with the virtue of roundness or perfection.[5]

The *I Ching*, or *The Book of Changes* has sixty-four possible combinations of trigrams. The book lists the meaning of each combination, which the individual must interpret in order to decide what to do. Professor Chen explains the role of man:

> According to the *Book of Changes* man is in a position to intervene in the course of events considerably beyond his own sphere. When, in accordance with the natural order, each thing is in its appropriate place, harmony is established. Now each situation demands the action proper to it, and in every situation there is a right and a wrong course of action; thus the individual comes to share in shaping his fate, for his actions intervene as determining factors in world events. At the center of events, the individual who is conscious of responsibility is on a par with the cosmic forces of heaven and earth, and in such a manner, can influence changes.[6]

4 Water War

INTRODUCTION

Gong the water god is an ancient destroyer god who wrestled for control of the earth shortly after the creation of people. His predecessor, Zurong the fire god, ruled the world peacefully before him. When Gong became the ruler, he wanted to expand his influence by increasing the amount of water in the universe—in the ratio of seven-tenths water to three-tenths dry land. To achieve his goal, Gong sent torrential rains and came close to destroying the world in a fierce power struggle with the fire god.[1] Nuwa, the creator of people, appears in this myth to counteract the two gods' destructive forces.

Although historically the two warring gods have most often been presented as giants, some paintings show Gong as having a snake's body and a human face with red hair. Zurong is traditionally shown with a massive human body featuring broad shoulders, red skin, and a red beard. Both gods have terrible tempers.

In ancient stories, the earth was seen as a flat square, and the sky was a dome held up at each of the four corners by a high mountain peak, one of which is the Buzhow Mountain, mentioned in the story. In reality, Chinese mathematicians had already calculated that the earth was a sphere by the first century A.D., long before Gong the water god's first appearance in classical history texts.[2]

Water War

Gong the water god pummeled the world with incessant bouts of rain and floods. The deluges battered homes into piles of rubbish, and they toppled ancient trees. Great mountains crumbled and crashed into the swelling muddy rivers. Gong showed no mercy as thousands of people and animals perished on the soggy, bloated earth.

The other gods avoided Gong because his fury was so intense. They watched silently as their moats, villages, and temples were destroyed, one by one. Finally, Zurong, the fire god, decided that Gong had gone too far. Zurong was irritated by the other gods' cowardice, and he did not approve of his successor's plans to reshape the earth into water-heavy proportions.

So Zurong challenged Gong to regain control of the earth. Gong gladly met his rival in combat. As the two powerful forces wrestled each other across the firmament, the sky shook with thunder, and lightning flashed across the sky. For days, they grappled, wrestled, and pinned each other higher and higher in the skies until they finally cracked the dome of heaven.

When neither god could gain control, Gong challenged Zurong to restage their battle on earth. Zurong gladly accepted the challenge. Gong swept down to earth, placing legions of his strongest soldiers on a floating raft made of bamboo reeds. It was ablaze with flags, drums, and the cries of a thousand battle-thirsty men. The raft surged across the water, sending jagged waves breaking across the sea. Huge sprays of seafoam bubbled and frothed around the raft.

Zurong placed himself strategically in the path of Gong's warriors. As Gong's battle raft approached, Zurong blasted forth a huge, towering pillar of fire. The leaping flames were sucked into the hollow cores of the raft's bamboo poles, which burst into flame, plunging Gong's soldiers to their watery deaths.

Gong jumped off the burning raft and dove down into the sea. Quickly, the water god called forth all his loyal subjects: the giant turtles, shrimp, crabs, and lobsters of the waters. Out of the deep sea, monsters rose with huge horns and wings like bats. The water god smiled as he surveyed his mighty forces. Unlike his human army, these water warriors had their own protective armor. They lived in the sea and could not die by drowning. At Gong's command, they stirred up waves as high as mountains to quell the fire god.

Gong cried to his rival, "You cannot win this war. I am the superior force. Admit it! "

Although Zurong had no one on hand to help him, he retorted, "No, you will never be the superior force; you are nothing more than a cowardly tyrant." Then Zurong whirled and drew up all his strength. He inhaled every particle of heat, spark, and ember in his being, and blew out a blast of fire at the rebel warriors. The heat of his flames scorched and burned the sea creatures to cinders inside their own armor. The sea became a floating mass of grit, shell, and ash.

The mighty Gong was defeated, his army dead or dispersed. All the gods rejoiced in Gong's defeat. Humiliated, Gong fled to the west until he reached the Buzhow Mountain. In his rage, he rammed his head into the pinnacle. His blow splintered off the sharp mountain peak and sent it flying upward, punching a huge hole in the sky. The dome of heaven, already fractured from the gods' wrestling match, now cracked into a thousand

fissures surrounding the gaping hole. At once, deadly creatures from beyond the heavens swooped down through the darkness to descend upon the earth.

At the same time, the force of Gong's blow split open the crust of the earth. Exploding mountains spewed forth hot rocks to scorch the land. Liquid fire oozed from every crevice, and smoke belched from the cracked ground. While the unsteady earth rocked and lurched, forest fires raged, and mountain lakes burst their containing walls, sending more debris to the shattered villages below. All the gods, including Zurong, were stunned. But they were powerless to save their collapsing world.

As Nuwa watched the destruction taking place on earth, the goddess became furious. She raced to find rocks of five sacred colors—black, white, red, green, and yellow—and smelted them together in a huge bonfire. Using this sacred mixture, she began bit by bit to mend the hole in the sky. All the while, she cursed at the carelessness of the gods who had caused this devastation. Next, Nuwa scooped up miles and miles of river rushes and stuffed up every burning crack she could find. As their ashes settled in the crevices, the earth subsided. Nuwa ripped up more river rushes, willows, and branches to dam the bursting rivers. The waters, too, slowed down to a rumble and then flowed smoothly and swiftly to the sea. Then Nuwa salvaged the huge legs of a dead warrior turtle to hold up the sky, like pillars, in the four corners of the world. As she propped up the northwest corner, however, the earth tilted up in the west and slipped down low in the east, and try as she might, she was unable to level the sky.

Finally, Nuwa lashed together twelve bamboo reeds to make a flute. She shaped the instrument like the tail of the phoenix, the bird of peace. She taught the people to blow through the flute to create clear, soothing notes, and she told the people to have heart, for music from a bamboo flute can vanquish all fears.

Because of the carelessness of the gods, the unquiet earth still suffers and occasionally rumbles and breaks. Forever after, heaven and earth are tilted toward the northwest. That is why the moon and stars move in that direction and why the rivers of China plunge downward across the country to spill into the eastern sea.

QUESTIONS AND ANSWERS

Q: *Why did Zurong the fire god decide to fight with Gong the water god?*

A: Zurong felt that Gong was too destructive, and he disagreed with Gong's plan to change the earth's balance of water and land.

Q: *Who helped the water god?*

A: Gong was aided by men, then by giant turtles, lobsters, shrimp, crabs, and other sea monsters.

Q: *How did Nuwa repair the earth?*

A: She melted colored stones together and patched up the sky. She stopped up the cracks with river rushes, and dammed the rivers with branches.

Q: *What did Nuwa use to prop up the sky?*

A: She salvaged the legs of a dead warrior-turtle to prop up the sky.

Q: *What did Nuwa give the people and why?*

A: She gave them a bamboo flute in the shape of a phoenix's tail. Playing it would make them forget about the horrible things they saw.

Q: *What happened to the geography of China as a result of Gong's actions?*

A: China is tilted so that it is high at the northwest corner where the stars and moon pass through, and low at the southeast corner where the rivers run into the sea.

EXPERT COMMENTARY

The five sacred colors mentioned in the story are connected to five important earth elements: green=wood, red=fire, yellow=soil, white=metal, black=water. In their study of Chinese festivals, authors Carol Stepanchuck and Charles Wong write:

> The elements, which are five natural forces, work together in a cyclical order to represent periods of rise and decay, production and destruction. Wood prevails over earth; metal prevails over wood; fire over metal; water over fire; and earth over water.[3]

No single element is powerful enough to destroy all others. Nuwa restores order by balancing the forces of the universe. In his classic *Chinese Mythology*, Anthony Christie proposes the following interpretation:

> [T]he activities of the goddess [are] full of difficulties, but one thing is clear: her task is to restore order. . . . The commentators say that the ash of reeds is efficacious [effective] in the repair of breached dykes because reeds grow in water. It may be that the concept of reed (water) and ash (fire) is also seen as an expression of harmonious union *yin-yang*, of order and equilibrium.[4]

The phoenix is an important creature in Chinese mythology, second in rank only to the dragon. Poet Brian Katz describes her:

> The phoenix, feng huang, was the sacred fire bird. It was truly a magnificent creature to behold, and it had the features of several different animals. It had the head of a swan; the throat of a swallow; the beak of a chicken; the neck of a snake; the legs of a unicorn; the arched back of a turtle; and the stripes of a dragon. Its feathers were made up of the five sacred colors: black, white, red, green, and yellow.[5]

Author Derek Walters adds:

> [The phoenix] has many miraculous attributes, but not self-rejuvenation and does not possess the Arabian phoenix's propensity for self-immolation. . . . It feeds on bamboo seeds . . . and drinks from fountains of fresh water. It is one of the four emblems of royalty, usually associated with the Empress.[6]

The Chinese instrument in the story refers to the *sheng*, which has twelve to thirteen bamboo reeds lashed together like the tail of the phoenix. Chinese music experts T. C. Lai and Robert Mok explain its mellow sound:

> [A]lthough the ancient Chinese hit upon the idea of the pitch pipe, they had to rely on the singing of the [mythological phoenix] birds to fix the pitch.[7]

5 Yu Rebuilds the Earth

INTRODUCTION

The story of Yu the Great is based on a king of the same name who ruled in Chinese legend from 2205 to 2197 B.C. Like all demigods of ancient times, Yu the Great changes into different shapes whenever necessary, including the forms of bears, humans, and dragons. Unlike the demigods of ancient times, Yu is the first to pass on his status as ruler to his descendants and thus create a dynasty, or ruling family. He named his dynasty the Xia [She ah]. It still remains a mythical dynasty, since archaeological evidence has not yet proven its existence. The dynasty that followed, the Shang (1523–1027 B.C.), has a rich heritage of pottery, bronzes, and artifacts, which places it as the first historical dynasty of China.[1]

The Chinese dragon is not an evil creature. On the contrary, he brings rain and guards the lakes and waterways. He is a composite creature with the horns of a deer, the ears of a cow, the eyes of a lobster, the head of a camel, the whiskers of a cat, the body of a snake, the belly of a frog, the scales of a carp, the talons of an eagle, and the paws of a tiger. Dragons love to make vibrations in the sky by rolling huge pearls, creating thunder. Lesser dragons are used as riding steeds by the gods of heaven.

The ruling king in this story is the Yellow Emperor, a good leader who struggled with the mighty rivers that flooded the country each year. According to ancient myths, the Yellow Emperor had a pile of magic dirt that could absorb water. His grandson Kun stole the magic earth and dropped little balls of dirt wherever he went. The dirtballs swelled into huge, fertile mounds of soil as they absorbed water. The peasants then scooped up the fertile soil and spread it over their sopping fields. Kun also built dams to control the flooding of the country's unpredictable rivers. Unfortunately, the dams often burst and reflooded the land. When the emperor found out about the theft, he was furious and sent Zurong the fire god, now the chief executioner, to track down and kill his grandson Kun. Zurong chased Kun to the ice glaciers of the Arctic and struck him dead with a flaming sword. Kun's body lay trapped and frozen in the ice.

Yu Rebuilds the Earth

Three years later, the Yellow Emperor sent Zurong the fire god to check on his grandson Kun's body. When he reached the spot where Kun was buried in the ice, the fire god was amazed to find that Kun's body was perfectly preserved in the ice. As he hacked open the glacier with his sword, Zurong accidentally split open Kun's body. A huge dark dragon flew out of the corpse. Terrified, Zurong fled to warn the Yellow Emperor. The huge dragon became Yu the Great, son of Kun, who was born with all the memories and knowledge of his father.

Like his father, Yu was filled with compassion for the farmers. However, unlike his father, he did not wish to incur the wrath of the Yellow Emperor. Immediately, he hurried to the Yellow Emperor's court. Bowing before the ruler, Yu pleaded for the lives of the farmers, "Your majesty, I beg you to pity the people for their suffering. Please help them restore their land." The Yellow Emperor was not impressed with Yu's pleas. He bellowed, "Do not forget that your father stole my magic earth and tried to restore the land without my permission!"

Yu replied, "Then give me some magic earth and your permission, and allow me to complete my father's work." Secretly, the Yellow Emperor agreed that the world was a big, muddy mess. None of his gods had any ideas about how to stop the raging rivers that flooded the country year after year.

Kun had tried to divert the rivers with dams but had failed. Therefore, every spring, the rivers continued to burst their banks, drown innocent people, and destroy property. Furthermore, the emperor was pleased that Yu had asked for the magic earth, rather than attempt to steal it. At last, the emperor said to Yu, "Pile the magic dirt on the back of this tortoise and go forth to control the floodwaters. With the help of this tortoise and a winged dragon, rebuild the world in your father's vision."

Yu was curious about the size and shape of the earth. Therefore, before leaving the emperor's court, he dispatched one of the lesser court gods to measure the country north/south and another god to measure the country east/west. Each returned to report exactly the same number: 233,500 *li* (three *li* make one mile) and 75 paces. Delighted, Yu created a map from the gods' descriptions, which made the earth a perfect square. Then Yu divided the country into nine areas, or provinces. Only then did he begin his construction work.

Unlike his father, Yu was not content merely to build dams to control the rivers. Instead, he studied the shape of the land in each area. He observed the course of the rivers and planned their most natural route to the sea. To guide the rivers, Yu dug canals, carved tunnels, leveled hilltops, created dams, and formed lakes. In each area, Yu used the tail of the dragon to gouge out new channels for the rivers.

As he plodded across the country, Yu found 233,559 large holes in the earth. Year after year, water had bubbled up in these cavities and flooded the world. Now Yu plugged up the gaping holes with dirt and reeds, and dropped in magic dirt balls from the tortoise's back to dry up the soggy earth caused by the floods.

When he worked, Yu often used the form of a human to avoid frightening the farmers. Even in his human form, he had

an ugly face like an insect, with a mouth like the bottom of a crow's beak and a long neck like a snake. The farmers did not care about his appearance, however. They loved him for his efforts on their behalf.

As Yu traveled across China, he named the tribal groups and recorded their customs: Leather-Skin people; Goat-Fur people; Oyster-and-Pearl people; Kingfisher-Green-Silk people; Grass-Skirt people; Felt-Tent people; Mountains-of-Jewels people; Dew-Drinkers; Red-Grain-Growers; Lacquer-Makers; Winged people; Short people; Deep-Set-Eyes people. He charted their land and collected samples of their soil as he traveled across the fifty rivers and mountains of China.

Wherever he went, Yu found happy families. Their happiness only made him aware of his own loneliness. Although Yu was married briefly, his wife and son both abandoned him because they had no fondness for digging dirt. With neither wife nor son by his side, Yu continued his work alone, with only the tortoise and the dragon for company. His hands were covered with sores and calluses. His skin was blackened and blistered from the sun. One leg shriveled and twisted as Yu limped around the rough terrain. Wherever he traveled, farmers hailed him as the Great Yu.

Their widespread affection caused the ruling emperor to choose Yu as the next emperor. It was thus that Yu became the founder and ruler of the Xia [She ah] dynasty. Soon plentiful grain harvests blessed the land. The rivers ran peacefully to the sea and did not overflow. The people lived happily in their villages and blessed the name of Yu in their joy and contentment.

QUESTIONS AND ANSWERS

Q: *How did Yu the Great come into being?*

A: Zurong the fire god was sent by the Yellow Emperor to check on his grandson Kun's body, which lay frozen in the ice. When Zurong hacked open the ice in which Kun's body was buried he accidentally split Kun's body in two. A huge dragon emerged, which became Yu the Great.

Q: *How was Yu successful in persuading the Yellow Emperor to allow him to repair the earth?*

A: Yu asked for the magic earth and did not steal it. The emperor was already sorry that the earth had reflooded, but before Yu, he did not have anyone who was capable of repairing it.

Q: *What did Yu do before he started his work?*

A: First, he sent gods to measure the earth. Then he tried to figure out the natural course of the rivers so he would not have to fight against their natural routes to the sea.

Q: *Who were Yu's companions and helpers?*

A: A dragon and a tortoise.

Q: *What did Yu do with the different tribes that he met?*

A: He gave them names, recorded their customs, charted their land, and collected samples of their soil.

Q: *Why were people not afraid of Yu's appearance?*

A: Most of the time, he appeared in the form of a human being. Farmers did not mind his ugly physical appearance because he worked so hard to reshape the country and restore their lands.

Q: *Why was Yu lonely?*

A: His wife and son abandoned him because they hated his earthy line of work.

Q: *Why were the people grateful to Yu?*

A: He devoted his life to helping the farmers, even at the expense of his own happiness. When Yu was emperor, the people were at peace and no one starved.

Q: *Why is Yu the Great a beloved myth?*

A: People liked to hear how their earth was formed and how the gods helped people inhabit their world.

EXPERT COMMENTARY

The Yellow Emperor may have been based on a real ruler of 2697–2598 B.C. Poet and author Brian P. Katz describes his reign and appearance in mythology:

> The development of time-telling devices, compasses, calendars, and coinage are all attributed to him. In one depiction, Huang Ti [the Yellow Emperor] is seen as monstrous: he has an iron head, a bronze brow, hair like swords, the body of a bull, and six arms with eight fingers each.[2]

The father and son pair of Kun and Yu are typical of the early mythological gods in their willingness to help people. Noted sinologists Jan and Yvonne Walls write:

> Characteristic of classical Chinese myths is their rather dominant concern with some of the universal themes–the creation and maintenance of natural and cultural orders, disruptions and challenges to them–and a spirit of concern and even self-sacrifice for the well-being of humanity on the part of benevolent gods and mythological culture heroes. . . . [T]he number of gods and culture heroes who give their lives in the service of the natural or cultural orders is astounding in comparison with most other pantheons: Pan Gu [Panku], Nü Wa [Nuwa] . . . and the god Gun [Kun] are examples to be found in this collection.[3]

The Walls continue:

> In the classical Chinese scheme of things, then, there was no place for a "jealous" god who demanded the exclusive devotion of a chosen people in return for his help. The gods held the power to influence the seasonal cycles and the balance between wet and dry, but usually they only intervened to punish people for wicked behavior, or to relieve them from excessive suffering, and if one god acted with malice towards humankind, another god could be counted on to send down a culture hero to struggle on their behalf.[4]

The Xia dynasty of the Great Yu and his descendants lasted for six hundred years and ended the period of the god-kings. With the next dynasty, the Shang, came recorded history and human rulers. Dr. John S. Major, director of the China Council of the Asia Society, explains the change:

> The square earth had to be drained, surveyed, marked out into its nine provinces, and set under the government of the flood tamer [Yu] himself. . . . [After the Xia dynasty] the world became familiar, ruled by a human emperor with a normal life span, and marked by the trouble and strife that is the lot of all mortals. For better or worse, we became masters of our own fate, but at a price–for the gods, those inhabitants of the celestial plane, withdrew from the plane of the earth, and were our constant companions no longer.[5]

6 The Grand Archer Yi

INTRODUCTION

In many ancient Chinese myths, as well as the myths of other cultures, the gods help the people. The Archer Yi, however, is one of the few mortals who helps the gods, thanks to his great skill with the bow and arrow. Like many of our previous tales, this story may have been based on an actual person, in this case a skilled bowman who lived sometime between 2436–2255 B.C.[1] Myths about him are linked to the people of the southwestern part of China.

Plants and herbs often appear in the background of Chinese stories. The mythical Fusang tree is reputed to be over ten thousand feet tall and spreads its leaves out over two thousand feet. Because the tree appears in many ancient tombs, paintings, and sculptures, it once must have been a very important symbol.

Although some versions of the story depict the Fusang as a hibiscus, the mulberry tree is probably its basis. One variety of the mulberry, *Morus alba*, is native to China. Growing more than fifty feet tall, its leaves are used to feed silkworms. Strands from the silkworms' cocoons are woven together to create silk, the strongest of all natural fibers. The cloth is lightweight and cool to the touch, but retains warmth and is highly flame-resistant. Its beauty and ability to absorb bright dyes made it a highly prized trade item in ancient Egypt, Rome, and Persia.

The water spinach, *ung choy*, has thick hollow stems and long slender leaves. It will sprout leaves and regenerate with very little water, and it will grow as much as four inches per day. This hardy plant saved people from starvation during China's many wars and is also a valuable source of iron for the people of India, Vietnam, Brazil, Central America, and Africa.[2]

The Grand Archer Yi

China was once thought to be surrounded by four seas. To the east was a vast ocean. Beyond the ocean, magnificent plants bloomed on an island paradise. The most glorious specimen of all the plant life was the Fusang tree, whose wondrous branches stretched up toward the heavens and out across the island for hundreds of miles. Scattered among its masses of dark green foliage, fragrant hibiscus flowers burst into flaming shades of magenta, crimson, and violet.

Among the glossy leaves of the Fusang tree lived ten naughty suns. They were left alone to play in paradise, neglected by their parents, the sun god Dijun and the sun goddess Shiho. Each day, Shiho left heaven in a pearl-shell chariot drawn by six fiery young dragons and passed by the Fusang tree. The suns took turns clambering to the treetop to leap into the chariot and make the rounds with their mother as she roared by. It was the job of each working sun, as the goddess Shiho wheeled her chariot across the sky, to shed light and warmth evenly across the world and wake up the roosters. But Shiho had to scold her sons constantly for fixing too much heat in places that captured their interest.

While one sun was on duty, the other nine frolicked among the jagged leaves of the Fusang tree. The suns spent idle afternoons happily chasing each other in the tree, then cooling themselves in the ocean. At dusk, they eagerly awaited their mother's chariot. The returning sun always splashed down in a series of splendid twirls and jackknifes to the noisy cheers of his brothers.

After many years, however, the suns became bored. All of them plotted to spend more time playing, and less time working. One day, they decided to run across the sky, all together, before their mother arrived. They hoped to generate enough light and warmth to last for several days. Then no one would need to work for awhile.

As the ten suns chased each other across the sky, the moisture on earth slowly evaporated. The light the sun brothers gave off together was blinding. Their heat scorched the soil, and rivers dried up to a trickle. Crops withered, and many people died of thirst across the land. There was nothing to eat except water spinach, which mercifully grew in the mud of their fields. Monsters appeared in the seas and skies to snatch the people from their homes. The people prayed to the gods night and day for deliverance. When their prayers finally reached the sun god Dijun, he became very angry at his sons' selfishness and laziness.

Dijun called the best marksman, the Grand Archer Yi, before him. The sun god gave Yi ten magic arrows. Then he ordered Yi to discipline his naughty sons. When the Grand Archer Yi saw all the dead creatures on the parched earth, he was filled with sadness, for he was a mortal man. Yi called out to the suns and ordered them to stop their foolishness, but they only leaped around the Grand Archer, mocking his seriousness.

When Yi threatened to shoot them with his magic arrows, the suns laughed even harder. They knew they were the sons of a god and that the Grand Archer was merely a heavenly court servant.

Angrily, the Grand Archer Yi grabbed one magic arrow out of his quiver and aimed carefully. Whaam! The arrow flew straight into the heart of the most boastful sun. Quickly, that sun dropped down from the sky, burning up in a ball of fire. When he hit the ground, the sun turned into a huge black crow with a three-foot wingspan, and then he died. The earth immediately felt cooler. Then the Grand Archer stalked the remaining suns.

Having witnessed Yi's powers, the other suns became frightened, and they scattered across the country, trying to hide. However, one by one, the Grand Archer tracked them down. Each time he killed one of the suns, the earth cooled further.

Zing! He shot the second sun and billowing clouds reappeared in the sky.

Zoom! He shot the third sun and mist curled around the high mountains.

Twang! He shot the fourth sun and dewdrops formed like pearls on every leaf.

Thump! He shot the fifth sun and springs bubbled out of the rocky hills.

Zap! He shot the sixth sun and rivers rippled with leaping carp.

Pow! He shot the seventh sun and branches sprouted lush green foliage.

Thud! He shot the eighth sun and buds blossomed on the trees.

Thwack! He shot the ninth sun and rice grass pushed up tender new shoots.

Then the Grand Archer Yi vowed to find the very last sun and bring him to justice.

By now, the land had cooled so dramatically that it was comfortable for the peasants. They wanted Yi to quit, but no one dared approach him. However, before the Grand Archer could spend his last arrow, a brave boy sneaked up behind him and stole the tenth shaft. After this show of courage, the peasants were emboldened enough to beg the Grand Archer to leave one sun to light up the heavens. Yi was filled with pity for the farmers, and he agreed to spare the last sun remaining in the sky.

This last sun mourned the loss of his brothers and was doomed to assume his daily journey alone. Furthermore, his mother rejected his pleas to borrow her chariot, and the dragons refused to pull him. From one end of heaven to the other, the last sun trudged across the sky in solitude, bringing light and warmth to the world for all eternity.

Prosperity returned to the people. Crops grew again, the rivers slaked their thirst, and the animals bathed in the fresh water and clear sunshine. Last of all, the people gave thanks for one plant, the water spinach, that grew wild in the muddy waters, allowing the people to survive the time of the terrible drought caused by the thoughtless ten suns.

QUESTIONS AND ANSWERS

Q: *What did the goddess Shiho require of her ten sons?*

A: She made them pay attention, do their duty, and not gaze too long at any one place.

Q: *Describe the Fusang tree.*

A: It was a huge tree that grew on an island in the middle of the ocean, and its branches stretched for miles. It had fragrant magenta, crimson, and violet flowers and glossy leaves. It was the home of the ten suns.

Q: *What powers did the suns possess?*

A: They warmed the earth and gave the people light.

Q: *What harm could the suns do?*

A: When they failed to pay attention to their duties, they unleashed too much heat and light, scorching the earth and drying up the rivers.

Q: *What job did Dijun the sun god ask the Grand Archer Yi to do?*

A: Dijun asked the Grand Archer to discipline his unruly sons.

Q: *Why did the suns laugh at the Grand Archer Yi?*

A: They considered him a lowly court servant, whereas they were children of the gods.

Q: *Why was the last sun spared?*

A: The peasants needed one sun remaining to give them light and warmth.

EXPERT COMMENTARY

The Archer Yi was an important character in ancient mythology. Classical texts mention him frequently as a key figure. Pictures of him appear on many tomb sculptures, shooting at the ten suns. The Shang dynasty believed in ten suns. Professor Sarah Allen of Dartmouth College presents one explanation:

> When the Zhou [a dynasty that ruled from 1027–221 B.C.], who believed in one sun, conquered the Shang, the myth lost its earlier meaning . . . people continued to believe in ten suns which rose in sequence from the branches of the Mulberry [Fusang] Tree in outlying regions. In the central states, this tradition was known but the ten suns were confined to the mythical past by the story that one day all of them came out at once and nine were shot by Archer Yi.[3]

The sun god Dijun plays only a small role in Chinese mythology. Professor Anne Birrell surmises:

> [T]he myth of the flood and its control was more nearly relevant to the lives of the people than the less real myth of the unnatural phenomenon of solar disaster.[4]

Dijun's wife Shiho plays a more prominent part in her position as mother of the suns. Scholar Anthony Christie clarifies:

> Both sun and moon are in fact suns and moons, ten and twelve in number respectively. Each of these heavenly bodies is in the care of a mother who is in some sense responsible for their proper functioning.[5]

Professor Birrell explains further:

> Ti Chun [Dijun] is one of the supreme gods, but in the evolution of myths he became a faded deity. . . .[6]

Jan and Yvonne Walls explain the fate of the balls of fire which fell from the sky after being hit by Archer Yi's arrows:

> Nine three-legged ravens had fallen to the ground. But where did all the fire balls go? It was said that they all fell into the vast ocean east of the sea to form a giant rock forty thousand *li* thick and forty thousand *li* in circumference. It was called "Wo Jiao" (The Fertile Scorch). Sea waters that dashed upon it would evaporate and disappear instantly. This is the main reason why, even though all the waters or all the rivers and streams empty into the sea, the sea never overflows.[7]

Water spinach is a nutritious plant. *Agricultural Research* magazine reports:

> The first historical record of cultivated water spinach, *Ipomoea aquatica*, comes from the Chin Dynasty. . . . Originating in India and Southeast Asia, the plant is rich in iron, making it an ancient remedy for anemia.[8]

While it is a highly prized vegetable in many parts of the world, the Weed Science Society of America warns of its potential for clogging up the waterways:

> A single plant can branch profusely and can grow to more than 70 feet in length. . . . Under ideal conditions [in Hong Kong], annual yields of the plant are up to 40 tons per acre.[9]

> It is known by many names: Water spinach, swamp morning glory, water convolvulus (United States); *ung choy* (Chinese); *kankoong* (Java); *balangoog* (Philippines); *rau muong* (Vietnam); *phakbong* (Laos); *tra kuon* (Cambodia); *nali* (India); *batillia acuatica* (Latin America).[10]

7

The Moon Goddess

INTRODUCTION

The moon goddess is a popular folk tale that dates from the Tang dynasty (A.D. 618–906).[1] Each province in China has its own version of her story. She is connected to the mid-autumn festival, a harvest celebration that occurs in mid-September.

When the Archer Yi shot down the nine suns, the sun god Dijun banished him. Dijun had expected Yi merely to discipline, not to kill, his sons. In addition to the Archer Yi, Dijun also banished Yi's goddess wife, Chang-O, to the earth below. The banishment suited Yi because he was regarded as a hero on earth, but Yi's wife was lonely for her sister goddesses and missed the luxuries of heaven. Chang-O was also angry at her husband for jeopardizing her social status. Therefore, although the Archer and his wife loved each other deeply, they often quarreled.

In order to keep their bodies in perfect condition, every three thousand years, gods must eat the peach of long life and drink the elixir of immortality from the Garden of the Western Paradise. This garden is tended by the Queen Mother Hsi Wang Mu [She Wong Muh], an old woman who has the fangs of a tiger and the tail of a panther. She lives alone and is protected by birds of prey and fearsome beasts. She also controls plagues and evil spirits. However frightful her appearance and her powers, Hsi Wang Mu is a motherly figure to all the gods in heaven.

In her enchanted garden grow the coveted peaches which she plucks and serves at a sumptuous banquet for the gods. She is an alchemist, or a person who practices the art of combining substances that will transform. Hsi Wang Mu can mix many elixirs, or magic potions, including the one that will insure immortality for the gods. In more recent versions of the story, the Queen Mother is shown as a graceful elderly woman.

The fabled Garden of the Western Paradise is thought to reside in a remote section of the Kunlun Mountains. These spectacular peaks are located in western China between Tibet and Xijiang and soar as high as twenty-five thousand feet. In mythology the mountains are the home of the Chinese gods, as well as the site of life-restoring herbs. Historically, the Kunlun range was part of the Silk Road, a caravan route between China and Persia used for trading silks, spices, and gold.

The Moon Goddess

Because he loved his wife very much, the Grand Archer Yi reluctantly set out on a journey to the Kunlun Mountains where the peaches of long life were grown by Hsi Wang Mu, the Queen Mother of the Western Paradise. The Archer was unsure of the road, and even less sure of how much strength he had left. When he lived in heaven, Yi had always ridden in the empress's chariot or straddled the tails of sky dragons to reach the Western Paradise, but now that he lived on earth, he had to walk. He crossed burning deserts, forded cold streams, and trekked over high mountains for thousands of miles.

Finally, Yi arrived at his destination and was greeted by Hsi Wang Mu. When Yi told her that his wife wanted a dosage of the elixir of immortality, Hsi Wang Mu could only sigh. Unfortunately, she told Yi, the gods and goddesses had just feasted on the last batch of peaches. The next peach crop would not ripen for another three thousand years. When Yi continued to implore her, Hsi Wang Mu took one leftover, very imperfect dried-up peach, pounded some herbs and powders, and stirred them together into an elixir. Then the Queen Mother poured the precious liquid into a small vial. "This potion will take both of you to the heavens. But make sure you take it on a clear night, or you could be trapped halfway between earth and heaven," she warned.

Carefully, the Archer placed the vial in his leather pouch and knotted the bag tightly around his waist. Again, Yi trudged over the same high mountains, forded the same cold streams, and crossed the same burning deserts to return to his wife. When he lived in heaven, he had not cared about its comforts and luxuries. Because of his status there as a mortal who served the gods, Yi, too, had been invited to sumptuous feasts and had eaten the peach of immortality. The magical potion had enhanced his already powerful body and made him invincible. Now on earth, however, he felt his power slipping day by day. Although Yi did not resent his banishment to earth, he was beginning to resent his decaying mortal body.

When at last the Archer returned home and presented the precious elixir to his wife, Chang-O was delighted. She burned with the anticipation of returning to her sisters in the sky. The goddess begged him to take the medicine immediately, but her husband refused, remembering the warning he had been given by the Queen Mother. Yi said, "I have undertaken a long journey to fulfill your deepest desire. We must be patient and wait for a clear night when the stars can guide us homeward."

Chang-O agreed with her husband's clear reasoning, but her desire to be reunited with her sisters was far stronger than her appreciation of his logic. When her husband left for his daily hunt, the goddess stared at the elixir. As the day and night wore on, Yi did not return. As was often the case, Chang-O spent the lonely night waiting for her husband's return. The Archer often stopped to chat with his neighbors to whom he gave generous portions of deer, rabbit, quail, pheasant, and duck from his hunt.

Chang-O sighed. The goddess knew by its smell that the elixir was already diluted. The dosage was so weak, she reasoned, that the Archer would probably never recover his full

strength by drinking his portion, and she would probably never regain her full beauty by drinking hers. Furthermore, they might never even reach heaven.

With these fears in mind, the goddess developed a plan. She would drink both of their portions so that she could return to heaven first, and beg the sun god to forgive her husband for his brashness in having shot down the nine suns. Then she and her sister goddesses could borrow some sky dragons to visit the Queen Mother of the Western Paradise. There, they would persuade her to mix up another dose of the elixir solely for the Archer so he could join his wife in heaven.

As she swallowed the elixir, Chang-O felt its bitterness burn her throat. Immediately, her body became lighter, and she felt dizzy. As she ran out into the night, her body floated upward to the stars. Unfortunately, the night was not clear. Chang-O wandered among the stars and lost her way. She finally came to rest, trapped in the cold moon.

The Archer Yi was just returning when he saw his wife drifting up to the sky. He called out to her and ran after her shadow, but she was too far away to hear him. Yi was heartbroken and wept for days. No one could console the grieving hunter.

The gods took pity on the Archer. Yi had served the gods well and always did their bidding faithfully. The Archer never complained about the countless petty tasks assigned to him by the lesser gods of heaven. Furthermore, Yi had saved the earth from droughts and monsters when the gods could not be bothered.

Therefore, once a year, the gods grant the Archer the right to ascend to the skies to be with his wife. On that one night, the harvest moon shines the brightest and fullest of the year, reflecting the Archer Yi's love for Chang-O.

QUESTIONS AND ANSWERS

Q: *Why was the Grand Archer Yi banished from heaven to live on earth?*

A: The sun god Dijun was angry at him for shooting down and killing the nine suns.

Q: *Why did Chang-O want to return to the stars?*

A: She missed her goddess sisters and the luxurious life of heaven. She did not like to feel her body dying on earth, and wanted to regain her youth and beauty.

Q: *What warning did the Queen Mother of the Western Paradise give to Yi?*

A: She warned the Archer Yi to drink the elixir on a night that was clear, or the drinker would be trapped halfway between the earth and heaven.

Q: *What was Chang-O's plan upon her return to heaven?*

A: Chang-O wanted to ask the sun god to forgive her husband. Then she would travel with her sister goddesses to obtain another dose of the elixir for Yi so that he could rejoin her in heaven.

Q: *Why didn't Chang-O obey the warning?*

A: She was too impatient to wait for a clear night. She knew the elixir was too weak to allow both her and her husband to return to the heavens. She thought she had a better plan.

Q: *What happened to Chang-O when she failed to heed the Queen Mother's warning?*

A: She lost her way among the clouds and was finally trapped in the moon.

Q: *Why did the gods take pity on the Archer Yi?*

A: He had always been a good court servant and did what he was told without complaining. And he had saved the earth from droughts and monsters. The gods also knew that he loved his wife very much.

Q: *What compromise did the gods make to reward the Archer?*

A: Once a year, on the night of the harvest moon, the gods allowed the Archer Yi to visit his wife in the skies.

EXPERT COMMENTARY

The moon goddess's popularity stems from her association with a very important harvest celebration. Anthropologist Roy Willis states:

> Most Chinese have a sentimental attachment to the moon, and particularly to the full moon, whose round shape symbolizes the reunion and completion of the family circle. The Mid-Autumn Festival, which is held on the fifteenth day of the eighth month in the lunar calendar, when the moon is full, is still very popular. On that evening families come together and, among other things, eat round "moon cakes."[2]

Derek Walters, Europe's most prolific author on Chinese culture, writes:

> At that time, for meteorological reasons, the full moon (the "harvest moon" to Westerners) always appears much bigger than usual. It was customary to have Moon-Watching parties, and offerings are still made to the Moon . . . and paper lanterns are in abundance. The autumn equinox marks the time of the year when nights become longer than the days, and as the Moon symbolizes the Yin, or feminine force, the rituals are performed by women, who offer incense and food at altars in the open air.[3]

Mythology expert Alexander Eliot points out the universal fascination with lunar myths:

> Lunar mythologies are often even more dramatic [than solar myths]. For while the sun always remains the same, the moon waxes and wanes—disappearing, only to come to life again after three moonless nights.[4]

Hsi Wang Mu is a constant presence in Chinese myths. Professor Anne Birrell comments:

> [S]he is polyfunctional and ambiguous. Moreover, her attributes and functions evolve over the centuries in accordance with the

changing values of myth in society. Thus she moves with relative ease from the role of wild and savage deity, the avenging goddess, to cultured and humanized queen, the audience-granting monarch. . . . The major attribute of the Queen Mother of the West is her power to confer immortality, and it is this that comes into play in the later mythological and literary tradition.[5]

Professor Tao Tao Liu of Oxford University tells of a version where the goddess chose, rather than was condemned, to reside in the moon:

Although Chang-O was now a goddess again [after swallowing the elixir], she did not know where to go to enjoy her immortality. She could not go back to heaven, for the inhabitants there rejected her because of her behaviour to her husband. Instead, she chose to go to the moon, which was uninhabited by anyone except a rabbit. . . . There she went and lived in cold splendour, and became known as the goddess of the moon.[6]

8

The Unicorn's Prophecy

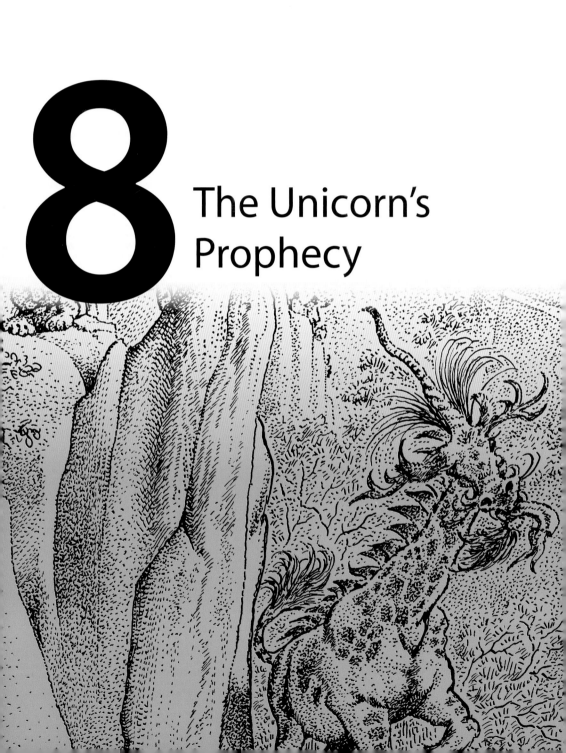

INTRODUCTION

Confucius was a real man, a famous teacher who lived between 551 and 479 B.C. His birth name was Kung Qiu [Kung Chew]. The word *Confucius* is a translation of "Master Kung," the name given to him by his followers. As was true for many other Chinese historical figures, myths such as the Unicorn's Prophecy sprang up around Confucius's life.

At the time of Confucius's birth, China was in chaos. Poor people had no way to improve their lives. Confucius introduced a system of beliefs to change the country. This system, which came to be called Confucianism, was based on a few simple ideas: Rulers could not force others to do their bidding, but instead should lead by persuasion and good example.

Many of Confucius's ideas were revolutionary for his time. For a brief period, Confucius was given a minor government job which he administered brilliantly. However, despite his success as an advisor to royalty, corruption in the royal household soon forced him out of his position. He was never again able to persuade the lords and princes of his time to overlook his humble beginnings and judge his ideas on their own merit.[1]

Confucius spent the rest of his life teaching and rewriting the classical literature of China. His followers kept his teachings alive after his death. In A.D. 59, more than four hundred years after his death, Confucius was recognized as a heavenly being by the emperor of the Han dynasty. Emperors adopted his ideas about good government and built schools in his honor.

This story introduces the unicorn, the Chi-lin [Chee leen], an animal sacred to the Chinese. It does not resemble the unicorn in European myths, but is a combination of many animals, including the deer, ox, dragon, and horse. A peaceful, timid animal, the Chi-lin left the innocent alone, but when angered, gored evil people with its horn. Trustworthy soldiers and fair judges wore the emblem of the Chi-lin on their clothing to remind them of their duties. In the fourteenth century, a real giraffe was sent to the imperial court, and many observers claimed it was the reincarnation of the mythical Chi-lin.

Chinese Mythology Rocks!

The Unicorn's Prophecy

Once there was a very kind woman named Cheng who lived in Shandong province in northwestern China. Loved and respected by everyone, she longed desperately for a child. Night and day, she prayed for a son. However, her husband scolded her for wanting another mouth to feed. Once he had been a nobleman, but he had lost all his money. Afterward, all his old friends avoided him and he became deeply ashamed of his poverty. Luckily, Cheng was willing to marry him.

One day, Cheng undertook a long journey to a remote temple to pray for a child. Her husband angrily refused to accompany her. The villagers all admired her bravery for attempting the journey to such an isolated place.

The trail was steep and rocky. Cheng felt alone in the world as she wound her way around the narrow, stony path. Her chest hurt as she breathed the cold, thin mountain air. In her pocket quietly jingled a string of coins, her meager earnings from selling embroidery in the market. She hoped to buy prayers, incense, and fruit for the temple goddesses.

Cheng had to dodge branches and avoid disturbing the rocks in the road. She was careful to tread lightly on the ground because she wanted to make as little noise as possible. She did not want to attract the attention of hungry tigers that roamed the hills, ready to pounce on easy prey. Even worse, bandits might find her. Once, these robbers had been hardworking farmers, but greedy lords took their crops, taxed them, stole their wives, enslaved their children, and took their land. After years of humiliation and starvation, the farmers' hearts turned to stone. Desperate and famished, they turned into robbers who roamed the countryside, stealing food and killing people. Over the years, the bandits had become more ruthless than any wild beast in the mountains.

As Cheng walked carefully along the dirt path, she stepped in some faint animal footprints. As she looked at them, the image of the footprints grew stronger and clearer. They were shaped like horse's hooves, only much larger. As she examined the hoof prints closely, her heart filled with joy. Could these be the footprints of the magic unicorn, the Chi-lin?

From childhood stories, Cheng knew that the Chi-lin appeared as an omen of peace. But her world was anything but peaceful. Poor people had known only fear, warfare, and strife.

As the woman continued to gaze at the mysterious footprints on the ground, a warm breeze swept over her body. She heard a light rustling of leaves, and a beautiful creature stepped forward from the trees. It was fifteen feet tall and covered with a pale yellow hide. Large spots like dark red clouds and purple mists covered its deer-shaped body. On its head, a single skin-covered fleshy horn sat between its ears. At its rear, a long tail switched gently to and fro like an ox's. Its horselike hooves stepped lightly on the earth so that it harmed no living creature. Its dragonlike neck moved in a slow, stately, fluid rhythm. Its large black eyes were as soft as wet dew. Indeed, it was the Chi-lin, the magic unicorn, walking toward her.

The woman watched the unicorn with a mixture of fear and awe. The beautiful creature approached the woman and stopped before her. To Cheng's surprise, the Chi-lin bowed its

head and dropped a piece of jade from its mouth at the woman's feet. When the creature spoke, its voice was like a clear, soft, faraway monastery bell. The Chi-lin told Cheng that soon she would bear a son who would be a great ruler, but one without subjects, a king without a throne. Then the unicorn bowed gracefully and disappeared back into the shadows of the trees.

Carefully, Cheng picked up the piece of jade. The Chi-lin's message puzzled her, and the lustrous jade seemed to hold deep secrets below its cloudy surface. The stone felt naturally cold, yet warmed up quickly in the palm of her hand. The jade appeared dense and cloudy, yet the longer she looked at it, the clearer and more transparent it seemed. Jade was harder than the bronze coins in her pocket, yet Cheng knew it could be carved into fluid shapes like twisting dragons, chirping insects, and tumbling clouds. When she struck the wonderful stone, the jade emitted a low-pitched musical note that inspired comfort and hope in Cheng's heart.

Cheng fervently hoped that the unicorn would bring peace to the troubled world. She rushed home to tell her husband about the magical encounter, her footsteps scattering the stones that she once carefully avoided.

True to the unicorn's prophecy, Cheng rejoiced at the birth of a son one year later. Cheng named him Kung Qiu. She placed the unicorn's jade around his neck to protect him against diseases and accidents.

Three years after the child's birth, Kung Qiu's father died, and the boy was raised by his mother in poverty deeper than ever before. Gifted with an exceptional memory, Kung Qiu remembered everything that he saw and heard. The boy loved to read and recite passages from classical literature. Despite his amazing intellect, or because of it, Kung Qiu was constantly teased as a child. He was not handsome and had a high, broad, protruding forehead. By the time the boy grew up, he was a giant, almost seven feet tall.

Kung Qiu had many good ideas. Unfortunately, no lords paid attention to him because he was poor. However, he decided to teach his beliefs to anyone who would listen. He was a powerful speaker, and he attracted a loyal following of three thousand people who called him Master Kung. His beliefs taught people how to behave decently toward each other.

> To learn without thinking is fatal, but to think without learning is just as bad.
>
> Do not worry if no one knows you, but be worthy of being known.
>
> A good man can influence those above him: the inferior man can influence only those below him.
>
> Do not do to others what you do not wish done to you.

Master Kung, the giant, had indeed fulfilled the unicorn's prophecy. He was a king without a throne, a ruler without a kingdom. Yet his ideas were true to the spirit of the Chi-lin, and they brought order and peace throughout the land.

QUESTIONS AND ANSWERS

Q: *At the time of Kung Qiu's birth, what were conditions like in China?*

A: Bandits robbed and killed people, and no one could stop them. Poor people were starving. The greedy lords took the farmers' crops, wives, children, and land.

Q: *What did the unicorn look like?*

A: It was tall and graceful with the body of a deer, the hooves of a horse, the tail of an ox, and the neck of a dragon. Its body was covered with a yellow hide with dark red and purple spots. It had one fleshy horn in the center of its head.

Q: *Why did Cheng think the unicorn might be a good omen for the people of her land?*

A: The Chi-lin was known as an omen of peace. People believed that it punished the evil and spared the innocent. It reminded judges and soldiers of their obligations to be fair.

Q: *What did the unicorn drop at the feet of Cheng, and what did it tell her?*

A: It dropped a piece of jade at Cheng's feet and told her that she would bear a child who would be a ruler without subjects, a king without a throne.

Q: *What are some special qualities of jade?*

A: Jade is a stone that has opposite qualities. It is a cool stone, but feels warm to the touch. It is heavy, but feels light in the hand. It is dense, but can be carved into light sculptures. Its surface is cloudy, but it has depth. It emits comforting sounds when struck. It has yin and yang elements. In this story, it was a gift from the unicorn to Cheng and her son.

EXPERT COMMENTARY

To describe China at the time of Confucius's birth, Professor William Edward Soothill from the Imperial University in Shanghai writes:

> Confucius, then, was born into a troubled period. The barons more powerful than their nominal sovereign, encroached and made war upon each other, at the instigation of ministers more crafty and ambitious even than themselves. The suffering people were . . . dragged from their fields and set to forced labour at and for the pleasure of their rulers, and driven to battles and raids in which they had no interest and from which they derived no benefit.[2]

In the twentieth century, Confucius has been attacked by the Chinese government for his insistence on moral conduct and for ignoring the rights of women. Yet, Confucius's demand for educational opportunities and access to governmental jobs for the poor was a radical idea for his times. Professor Herrlee Glessner Creel of the University of Chicago argues:

> Tradition paints him as a strict pedant [teacher], laying down precise rules for men to follow in their conduct and their thinking. . . . He is often called a reactionary, whose primary aim was to restore the ways of antiquity and to bolster the authority of the hereditary aristocracy. In fact, he advocated and helped to bring about such sweeping social and political reforms that he must be counted among the great revolutionaries.[3]

The myth features jade, a stone of contrasts: cold, yet warm; hard, yet carvable; flawed, yet enchanting. Professor René-Yvon Lefebvre d'Argencé, a world-renowned art expert, elaborates:

> Already in Confucius' time, jade was the favorite stone of the perfect gentleman, because it embodied all the cardinal virtues. Its warm brilliance was likened to charity, its hardness to wisdom, the sharp yet harmless edges of its contours to justice.[4]

Imperfections such as veins, specks, mottling, calcifications, and uneven patches of color contributed to the stone's beauty rather than detracted from it. Professor d'Argencé explains, "Its flaws, that are obvious without impairing its beauty, were compared to loyalty and its translucency and radiance to honesty."[5] Pure jade is white, but chemicals and other minerals add colors and imperfections to the stone during its formation in the earth. Some colors are given especially descriptive names: snow jade, mutton-fat white, chicken-bone white, milky white, spinach green, apple green, kingfisher (emerald) green, cinnabar red, rust red, lavender, black, and blue.

Through the ages, jade has been used for ceremonial blades (axes, daggers and swords), religious containers and nature spirit figures (oxen, cicadas, doves, dragons, carp, mountain scenes), and, currently, for personal treasures (chopsticks, writing brushes, teacups, rice bowls, jewelry).

Professor d'Argencé sums up its symbolism: "With time jade came to be associated in popular belief with everything that is noble, pure, beautiful and indestructible."[6]

9 Monkey

INTRODUCTION

By the first century A.D., a philosophy called Taoism dominated Chinese thought. Taoism was based on the *Tao Te Ching* [dow deh jing], a collection of eighty-one verses written by the philosopher Lao-tzu. The *Tao Te Ching* puts forth the idea of following the Tao, usually translated as "the Way," the natural creative life force of the universe. It also speaks of noninterference, or *wu-wei*, with living creatures and forces.

From a philosophy, Taoism gradually grew into a religion. Temples were built, and monks were given the task of overseeing these places of worship. The Taoist heaven was soon populated with a ruler, the Jade Emperor, who was assisted by eighty gods and goddesses. Likewise, hell was also ruled by an emperor, Yen-lo, with a host of demons to oversee its functions. Taoists became fascinated with immortality, spells, elixirs, alchemy, and magical powers such as flying and transformation (from one shape to another).[1]

Fifteen centuries later, a government official named Wu Ch'eng-en wrote a popular novel entitled *Journey to the West*. The following myth retells the first part of that novel. It features the most well-known character in Chinese folklore, the Monkey King. His exploits demonstrate Monkey's Taoist training and powers. He is vain, rude, and greedy, but Monkey's magic tricks and saucy personality make him a beloved character.

Monkey

On the Mountain of Fruit and Flowers, a magic rock gave birth to a stone egg. From this stone egg emerged a monkey whose first act was to jump up and bow to the four directions. His eyes flashed like lightning, and his teeth glinted like the stars at night.

He played with other monkeys and with wolves, tigers, and deer, but he had an enormous appetite and often gobbled up their share of grass, leaves, berries, and fruit. Still, his joyful personality and curious nature made him the most popular animal on the mountain.

One day, Monkey jumped through the waters of a cascading waterfall and discovered behind it a cave furnished with stone bowls, cups, and chairs. Delighted, Monkey called all the other monkeys to come see the novelties he had found. When they arrived, the other monkeys grabbed the utensils, made themselves comfortable in the cave, and proclaimed Monkey their king. Amidst the wild orchids and aromatic herbs growing in the mountains, the monkeys lived in perfect happiness for centuries.

But one day, the Monkey King burst out in tears. He realized that soon he might face Yen-lo, the King of Death. In response to his fear, he stole some clothes and sandals and went out to search for the secret of immortality. Everywhere he went, he imitated human speech and manners, but people just laughed at his strange costume: a red dress, a yellow sash, and black shoes. For ten years, he wandered from village to village until finally he found the cave of an immortal. After much pestering, Monkey was accepted as a disciple of this holy man.

From the immortal, Monkey learned to study the Taoist teachings, and to write and speak properly. He had to sweep the cave floor, gather firewood, fetch water, and tend the garden. After awhile, Monkey learned many tricks from the immortal. Now he could transform himself into seventy-two different trees, animals, and rocks. After much persuasion, the immortal also taught him how to fly, by soaring on the clouds. Once he mastered these skills, Monkey loved to show off in front of the other disciples. One day, the immortal caught him changing into a pine tree. Angered that Monkey would squander his valuable magic by showing off, the immortal promptly banished Monkey from the cave.

The First Return Home

So the Monkey King returned to his home on the Mountain of Fruit and Flowers. His subjects greeted him noisily, reporting that a demon was robbing their cave. Catching this demon had proven futile. Each time the demon had appeared, he had grabbed a few of their monkey children and held them prisoner until he was ready to eat them.

Immediately, the Monkey King issued a challenge to the demon. When the demon heard his cries, he laughed at the bellowing monkey. He put away his sword, and hurled himself at the skinny creature. The demon and Monkey fought for hours, dealing each other glancing blows, great jabs, and swift kicks. Finally, Monkey remembered one of the tricks he had learned from the immortal. Quickly, he pulled out a clump of hair from his head, bit the hairs into small pieces, spat them out in the air, and shouted "Change!" At once, the bits of hair turned into several hundred little monkeys, all of whom startled the demon with their piercing screams. The little monkeys pummeled the demon until they knocked him out. Then Monkey changed the little monkeys back into hair. He freed the imprisoned children and returned them to their parents. To celebrate their king's return, the cave monkeys feasted on dates, fruit, and grape wine.

The Visit to the Dragon King

Monkey decided that the demon was right to have laughed at him. He was king of his monkeys, but he did not have any clothes or weapons worthy of a king. So Monkey recited a spell and dove into the sea to meet with the Dragon King of the Eastern Sea. When he demanded a suitable weapon, the Dragon King showed Monkey a heavy iron pillar weighing several tons. No one in the sea could lift it; many feared its strange, glowing light. Monkey grabbed the stick, recited a spell, and changed it into a weapon-sized iron rod. Making thrusts and parries, Monkey jabbed and swung the stick in the air so ferociously that the tortoises drew in their heads, and the crab, shrimp, and lobster soldiers all scuttled out of his way.

But Monkey was not satisfied with the wonderful iron stick. Next, he demanded suitable clothing from the Dragon King. The Dragon King summoned his dragon brothers by beating on gongs and drums. From their treasuries, the dragons gave Monkey a pair of cloud-stepping shoes made of lotus fiber, a cap made of phoenix feathers, and a chain mail vest made of yellow gold. Without so much as a nod of thanks, Monkey left. The Dragon King and his brothers were angry at Monkey's poor manners and complained to the gods in heaven about the Monkey King's rude behavior.

When Monkey returned to his mountain home, he showed off his new clothes. He preened this way and that, and twirled around and around in front of the admiring monkeys. Then Monkey pulled out his iron staff. First he changed it into a long bridge that arched over the widest river; then he transformed it into a tall tower that touched the clouds. Finally, he shrank the iron staff into a tiny embroidery needle and tucked it behind his ear, grinning at his astonished subjects. With his fine clothes and new weapon, Monkey proclaimed himself the equal of any god in heaven.

Monkey Gets a Job in Heaven

Soon the gods in heaven became irritated with Monkey's behavior and decided to capture the insolent character. The gods convinced two demons from the Underworld to tie up Monkey and take him before the Ten Judges of the Dead. Monkey made a commotion and bitterly protested his capture. He demanded that the judges check the Ledger of the Dead, which recorded the life span of every creature on earth. As he upbraided the judges, Monkey quickly crossed out his name in the Ledger of the Dead with a thick black brush. Without his name in the ledger, the Underworld demons had no choice but to let him go.

Since the gods were unsuccessful in sending Monkey to the Underworld, the Jade Emperor decided to keep an eye on Monkey in heaven. He summoned the Monkey King and gave him the job of stable master. Monkey was to feed, groom, and water the thousand horses of heaven. Monkey was so insulted at having been given this menial job that he left in a huff and returned to his mountain cave. When heavenly court officials came to the cave to fetch him, Monkey put up such a fuss that they agreed to give him a more important job.

Monkey Creates a Mess in Heaven

Next, the Jade Emperor put Monkey in charge of the peach garden. Tiny fruit blossoms ripened into the sweetest peaches in the universe. These peaches would bestow wisdom, strong limbs, eternal youth, and light bodies to those fortunate enough to eat them. Greedy Monkey told his guards to stand outside his room while he napped. But instead of napping, he took off his bright robes and sneaked into the garden where he gorged himself on the ripe peaches. Then he curled up and fell asleep in the orchard.

Unbeknownst to Monkey, a great feast was being prepared for the gods. That afternoon, fairy maidens entered the peach garden to pick the fruit. To their dismay, they found many broken branches, peach pits, and a sleepy Monkey who berated them for disturbing him. When the fairies mentioned the great feast, Monkey suddenly realized that he had not been invited. The thought of rare meats, wine, and more fruit made the greedy monkey hungry again, and he dashed off in search of banquet tidbits.

Monkey sneaked into heaven's kitchen and knocked over steaming bamboo baskets as he stuffed himself with luscious meat dumplings. He then tiptoed into the wine cellar and quickly guzzled down several casks of wine, each more fragrant than the one before. In his haste, he accidentally tipped over some wine barrels and broke several casks. Monkey ran out into the night, fearing that the palace cooks would find him.

Looking for a place to hide, he stumbled into Tushita Palace, where the great philosopher Lao-tzu lived. Since the wise man was not at home, Monkey peeked at all the rooms in the philosopher's house. In the alchemy lab, Monkey found five gourds full of the elixir of immortality. On the table, almost a hundred pills, rolled out from the cooled elixir, were neatly lined up in rows, ready for the banquet. He scooped up a fistful

of pills and gulped them down like toasted soybeans, scattering the rest all over the floor. He dropped to his hands and knees and grabbed the remaining pills, turning over several tables in the philosopher's tidy workroom. Surveying the mess he had made in the alchemy lab, and remembering similar scenes of wreckage in the peach garden, kitchen, and wine cellar, Monkey decided to sneak out of heaven.

When he returned to his mountain home, the monkeys welcomed him with date wine, but having been spoiled by the fine wines of heaven, the Monkey King spat out their local brew. He boasted that he could bring back heaven's most delicious grape wines. Then Monkey quietly tiptoed back into heaven and stole the remaining casks. He brought the precious wine to his waterfall cave and celebrated his return to the Mountain of Fruit and Flowers.

When the Jade Emperor discovered the destruction, he sent his heavenly army generals to capture the thief. Monkey fought them with his embroidery needle, which he transformed into a mighty fighting stick. No one could defeat Monkey, not even the hundred thousand heavenly troops who fought him with axes, sticks, and swords. And so it was that the orphan Monkey, born of a stone egg from a magic rock, established his supremacy in the fighting arts.

QUESTIONS AND ANSWERS

Q: *Where is the story of Monkey taken from?*

A: The story is from a novel called *Journey to the West* written by a government official named Wu Ch'eng-en.

Q: *How was Monkey created?*

A: Monkey was born from a stone egg that came from a magic rock on the Mountain of Fruit and Flowers. When he emerged from the stone, he bowed in the four directions.

Q: *What qualities defined Monkey's personality?*

A: He was greedy, but joyful, curious, and extremely popular with the other animals.

Q: *What made Monkey afraid?*

A: He realized he would soon face Yen-lo, the King of Death.

Q: *What did Monkey learn from the immortal?*

A: He learned to study the teachings of Taoism, to write and speak properly, how to fly, and how to transform himself into other natural forms, such as trees or rocks.

Q: *How did Monkey defeat the demon who had been robbing his cave?*

A: He pulled out a clump of his hair and transformed the pieces into hundreds of little monkeys, who helped him defeat the demon.

Q: *What did Monkey seek from the Dragon King?*

A: He wanted new suitable clothing, shoes, and a weapon worthy of a king.

Q: *Why did the demons drag Monkey to the Underworld?*

A: He was so troublesome that the gods wanted to imprison Monkey in the Underworld. Also, according to the Ledger of the Dead, Monkey's time on earth was over.

Q: *What were Monkey's jobs in heaven?*

A: At first he was given the job of stable master and put in charge of heaven's horses. Monkey was so insulted that he left heaven, until the Jade Emperor gave him a more important assignment— to be in charge of the orchard of immortal peaches.

Q: *Why did Monkey search for banquet tidbits?*

A: Monkey was greedy by nature, and he wanted to taste the banquet meats, wines, and fruit. He was also insulted that he had not been invited to the feast.

Q: *What did Monkey steal to eat and drink?*

A: He consumed the magic peaches from the orchard, dumplings from the kitchen, wines from the heavenly cellar, and all the magic pills of immortality from Lao-tzu's house.

Q: *Who was Lao-tzu?*

A: He was a great philosopher, the author of the *Tao Te Ching*, and the founder of Taoism.

EXPERT COMMENTARY

Both the *Tao Te Ching* and *Journey to the West* are two well-known pieces of literature. Fatima Wu, assistant professor at Loyola Marymount University, explains the widespread affection for *Journey to the West* in China:

> If one is asked to name a Chinese book that is known to all ages and all social levels, one has to nominate *Journey to the West*. An illiterate in China might not have read it, but he or she must have heard about it or seen it performed on stage. The main characters, especially Monkey, have appeared in operas, cartoons, movies, juvenile books, and colloquial tales. In other words, it is a story that everyone knows about.[2]

The *Tao Te Ching* is an important piece of world literature. Russell Kirkland, associate professor at the University of Georgia, writes:

> It [the *Tao Te Ching*] is known throughout the world, for it has been translated into every major language on earth, and into many minor ones. There are over a hundred versions in English alone. In fact, the *Daode jing* [*Tao Te Ching*] has been translated more often into more languages than any other work in history except the Bible.[3]

Little is known about Lao-tzu except that he is credited with the authorship of the *Tao Te Ching*. In contrast, Lao-tzu's mythological beginnings are widely celebrated. Poet and translator Witter Bynner describes Lao-tzu:

> Immaculately conceived to a shooting-star, carried in his mother's womb for sixty-two years and born, it is said, white-haired, in 604 B.C., he became in due time keeper of imperial archives. . . . [S]addened by men's tragic perversity . . . Laotzu [Lao-tzu] rode away alone on a water-buffalo into the desert beyond the boundary of civilization, the great wall of his period.[4]

When he arrived at one of its gates, a guard stopped him and persuaded him to write down his thoughts. Lao-tzu lived another three hundred years to complete his eighty-one verses.

The Tao, or the Way, is often explained through the metaphor of water. Professor Kirkland paraphrases Lao-tzu:

> Specifically, the Tao is humble, yielding, and non-assertive. Like a mother, it benefits others selflessly: it gives us all life and guides us safely through it, asking nothing in return. . . . Water, for instance, is the gentlest and most yielding of all things, yet it can overcome the strongest substances and cannot itself be destroyed. More importantly, however, water lives for others: it provides the basis of life for all things, and asks nothing in return. If we learn to live like water does, we will be living in accord with the Tao, and its Power (De) will carry us safely through life. Such a way of life is called *wuwei*, usually translated as "non-action". . . . [O]ne should follow one's natural course and allow all other things to do likewise, lest our willful interference disrupt things' proper flow.[5]

10 The Pilgrimage

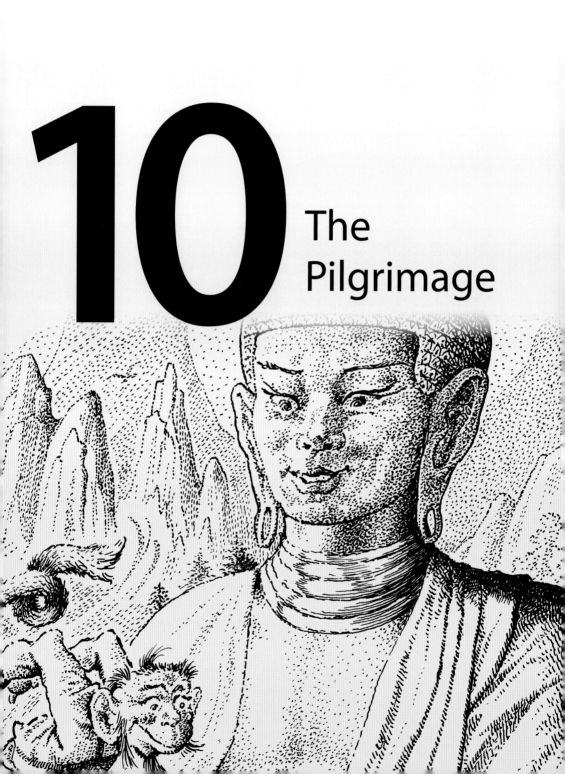

INTRODUCTION

The Buddhist religion was first introduced to China from India in A.D. 67. Its founder was Siddhartha Gautama, later known as the Buddha. He taught that suffering was caused by greed, which can be overcome by thinking quietly (meditating). When a person dies, he or she will be reborn into another life (reincarnation). This cycle of rebirth can only be broken when a person has lived an exceptionally good life and has given up the natural human bonds and attachments to material existence.

The novel *Journey to the West* was based on the travels of a real person, a monk named San Zang. Sometime during the Tang dynasty (A.D. 618–906), San Zang took a pilgrimage to India which lasted seventeen years. He risked his life many times for the purpose of bringing back the Buddhist scriptures to China. The fictionalized account of his travels, totaling eighty-one adventures, forms the greater part of the novel.[1]

Another important Buddhist figure, Kuan Yin, the goddess of mercy, appears in the story as a guide to San Zang and his pilgrim followers. She is very powerful and can "break the chains of prisoners, remove venom from snakes, and deprive lightning of its power."[2] Although the travelers are guided by the goddess Kuan Yin, they must use their own cunning to outwit the demons and dangers they encounter.

The previous chapter depicts Monkey's Taoist powers. In this chapter, Monkey converts to Buddhism, but he continues to use the knowledge gained from his Taoist training to combat evil.

The Pilgrimage

After Monkey outlasted the axes, sticks, swords, and lances of the gods, he boldly announced his plan to depose the Jade Emperor, the ruler of heaven. The gods and goddesses gasped at his audacity and whispered among themselves in shocked tones.

Finally, the Buddha stepped in. All the gods in heaven listened respectfully as he commanded the deities to stop fighting with Monkey. Then the Buddha asked Monkey why he wanted to replace the Jade Emperor. Monkey replied that his own clever magic spells and fighting ability made him superior to anyone in heaven, including the Jade Emperor. Monkey bragged about how he could transform himself into seventy-two types of animals, plants, and rocks. He boasted that his somersaults could take him through the clouds a hundred and eight thousand *li* to the end of the world.

The Buddha issued Monkey a simple challenge. "Jump across my palm and heaven is yours," the Buddha said. Monkey smiled when he saw that the Buddha's hand was no more than eight inches across from fingertip to wrist. Then Monkey took in a mighty breath and hurled himself through the air. When he landed, he saw nothing but five pillars holding up the world. Certain that he had somersaulted to the ends of the earth, Monkey laughed at how easily he had met the Buddha's challenge. Just to mark his spot, he took out a hair from his head and transformed it into a brush. With his finest calligraphy,

he wrote "Monkey, the great sage, reached this place." Then he somersaulted with great joy back to the palace, eager to claim the throne.

The Buddha smiled and showed Monkey the palm of his hand. There next to the middle finger were the miniature words "Monkey, the great sage, reached this place." Monkey realized that he had not reached the end of the world, but had merely jumped halfway across the Buddha's hand. The Buddha grabbed Monkey and sealed him inside a stone box high on a mountaintop. He left Monkey there, inside his stone box, for five hundred years.

Kuan Yin's Task

Meanwhile, China was full of greedy, mean, and quarrelsome people. Only a few had adopted the Buddha's teachings. The Buddha thought these teachings would encourage the people to behave more compassionately. However, he decided that if he gave away his scriptures, the people would not appreciate his words. Instead, the Buddha knew that the people must come to India to fetch the scriptures themselves. Furthermore, he wanted the Chinese emperor to finance the journey and urge his subjects to help the pilgrims all along their way. The Chinese people would value the Buddha's scriptures, if they were involved in helping to obtain them.

The Buddha summoned Kuan Yin, the goddess of mercy, to his home in India. She agreed with the Buddha that the journey to fetch the scriptures was necessary. People on earth desperately needed more spiritual guidance. However, because she recognized that the road between India and China was a dangerous one, Kuan Yin offered to travel it first, on foot, to map the route between the Buddha's home in India to the emperor's palace in China. At the same time she could also assess and confront the types of dangers that human pilgrims might encounter along the way. The Buddha agreed with Kuan Yin's plan.

The Sandy-Haired Monster, the Pig, the Dragon, and the Monkey

With an assistant, Kuan Yin recorded distances and the location of mountain paths along the road from India to the emperor's home in China. At a river crossing, a hideous sandy-haired monster jumped out and attacked Kuan Yin's assistant. When the monster realized that it was the goddess Kuan Yin standing on the shore, he bowed before her and confessed that he ate pilgrims who crossed his river. He tried to hide from her gaze the nine human skulls that he wore around his neck, as he begged the goddess for forgiveness. She invited the sandy-haired monster to repent by helping pilgrims instead of harming them.

As Kuan Yin continued on to a high mountain pass, a most horrible smell greeted her. Kuan Yin's assistant found a filthy pig with long tusks who attacked them with a rake. The pig stopped immediately when Kuan Yin tossed some lotus flowers between them. He recognized the goddess, and told her that once he had been a god. The pig begged her to help him return to his former life in heaven. Kuan Yin asked him to earn his way back to heaven by helping travelers instead of attacking them.

Next, Kuan Yin and her assistant were accosted by a dragon. Dragons are usually harmless spirits, but this dragon was deeply disturbed. He had accidentally set his father's kingdom on fire and destroyed some pearls of wisdom. While he waited anxiously for his execution date the doomed dragon assaulted travelers. Kuan Yin pledged to cancel the dragon's death sentence if he would reform. The dragon readily agreed and transformed himself into a white horse to assist any travelers on the deserted road.

When Kuan Yin came across the very last mountain range, she found Monkey encased in a stone box. Five hundred years had passed since the Buddha's challenge. Monkey was sorry that he had been greedy and arrogant. Like the others, he agreed to convert to Buddhism and offered his help to worthy pilgrims.

Tripitaka

Finally, Kuan Yin reached the palace of the earthly Chinese emperor. When she explained her mission, the emperor readily agreed to finance the journey to India. Like the Buddha and Kuan Yin, he was greatly concerned about the selfishness and greed of his people. If, as they hoped, the pilgrims were successful in their quest, the merit of the new religion could be proclaimed throughout the land. However, the emperor knew that wandering souls could easily be lost in the cold high mountains of the journey. Tigers, panthers, and snakes lurked in every forest. Stories of these fierce animals were terrifying, but people also trembled at tales of strange ghosts and spirits who could change their shapes at will.

When the emperor asked for pilgrims, no one stepped forward. At last, a humble monk named San Zang offered to fetch the scriptures. San Zang's fellow monks from the monastery were astonished that such an unassuming man would volunteer for such a dangerous mission. They expressed their fears for his safety. The brave monk replied that a sincere heart and his sacred vow to fetch the scriptures would shield him from harm. Like the Buddha, Kuan Yin, and the emperor, the monk was concerned about the lack of compassion he saw in his people. He hoped that the Buddha's teachings would help the people learn new and better ways of living.

The emperor was delighted that a brave pilgrim had at last been found. Because the scriptures were called *Tripitaka* in India, the emperor renamed the monk Tripitaka. As Tripitaka set out, the autumn air was beginning to chill the monk's bones, and a light frost covered the ground. Along the way, Kuan Yin guided the monk from afar, but she could not interfere with his decisions and actions.

Tripitaka joined up with Monkey, the dragon (in the form of a white horse), the pig, and the sandy-haired monster. All five set off for eighty-one adventures to fetch the holy scriptures from India. Time and again, they met dangerous ogres, monsters, and fairies who lay in wait. Because Tripitaka was a young Buddhist monk with a pure heart, evil spirits tried to corrupt him. Monsters wanted to eat his flesh.

Monkey used all his magical powers—flying, transformation, making himself invisible, acrobatics, and his embroidery needle cudgel—to defend the monk. He fought skeleton demons, giant spiders, and evil fairies in the shape of foxes. Monkey was boiled in oil, his head was chopped off (whereupon he simply grew a new one), and his stomach was cut open—but none of these vicious assaults produced any lasting harm.

When the pilgrims finally arrived in India, they were rewarded with the sacred scriptures. Then the five pilgrims returned to China with great joy. Now every person had access to the holy scriptures, and the people learned to set aside their greed and follow the way of the Buddha, as well as the way of the Tao. In this manner, they lived in harmony for centuries.

QUESTIONS AND ANSWERS

Q: *What was Monkey's new goal?*

A: His plan was to depose the Jade Emperor, who ruled heaven, and take his place.

Q: *What challenge did the Buddha issue to Monkey to test his worthiness to rule heaven?*

A: The Buddha told Monkey that if he could jump across his palm, Monkey could rule in heaven.

Q: *What did the Buddha do with Monkey when he failed to jump across his palm, and why?*

A: The Buddha sealed Monkey inside a stone box and left him high on a mountaintop for five hundred years. He did this to teach Monkey humility, and to give him time to meditate on his goals and priorities.

Q: *Why didn't the Buddha simply give his scriptures to the people of China?*

A: He wanted the emperor and the people to earn them, so that they would appreciate the knowledge the scriptures contained.

Q: *What plan did Kuan Yin propose to the Buddha?*

A: She would walk the route first between the Buddha's home in India and the Chinese emperor's palace, and make a map. That way the pilgrims would have a tool to help them find their way from China to India.

Q: *What evil characters did Kuan Yin encounter along her route, and what did they all decide to do?*

A: Kuan Yin met a hideous sandy-haired monster, a horrible-smelling pig, and a disturbed dragon. They all decided to help the pilgrims, if Kuan Yin would help them reverse their fates.

Q: *Whom did Kuan Yin meet on the very last mountain range?*

A: She found Monkey encased in his stone box.

Q: *How would a successful pilgrimage help the spread of Buddhism?*

A: People would see how powerful the new religion was if its pilgrims were able to survive their dangerous trip.

Q: *Who volunteered to fetch the scriptures?*

A: A humble monk named San Zang stepped forward for the dangerous mission. The emperor renamed San Zang "Tripitaka," after the Indian name for the scriptures.

Q: *Why did the Buddha, Kuan Yin, the emperor, and San Zang agree to the dangerous trip?*

A: They knew that the people were greedy and selfish, and that they needed some new religious ideas and spiritual guidance.

Q: *What happened to Taoism when Buddhism was introduced to China?*

A: The people of China were able to follow both the new teachings of Buddhism and the Way of Taoism.

EXPERT COMMENTARY

Dr. Daniel Overmyer of the University of British Columbia explains Buddhism's appeal:

> Wherever it went, Buddhism was accepted by many people as a new, liberating religion that had something for everybody; simple morality for peasants and sophisticated philosophy for intellectuals, all based on scriptural texts and interpreted by literate monks. As has happened with the founders of other religions, the Buddha came to be venerated as a superhuman being whose teaching was eternally true, even though one suspects such veneration would have made him uneasy.[3]

Kuan Yin also continues to hold a high place in the pantheon of Chinese gods. Martin Palmer, director of the International Consultancy on Religion, Education and Culture (ICOREC) states:

> Kuan Shih Yin, to accord her her full title, is the One who Hears the Cries of the World. She is the living expression of loving compassion; the one who will come to your aid; the one who offers a caring aspect to the otherwise somewhat remote world-view of much of Chinese Buddhism. . . . She will save you from the perils of this world and the next. . . . If you are desperate for a child, you turn to her, for she brings children. If you are sick, you turn to her for healing. If you are in danger, you pray to her for deliverance. She is all pervasive, all loving, the very embodiment of beauty and grace. It is hardly surprising that she is so popular.[4]

Although *Journey to the West* is the story of the introduction of Buddhism to China, it is also a reminder of the power of Taoism and Confucianism. In Palmer and Xiaomin's version, Monkey says:

> Now [that] we have defeated these evil beasts you must see there is a Way in the Buddhist teachings also. From now on do not take

one religion only, but honor both the Buddhist clergy and the Taoist Way, as well as educating intelligent men following the Confucian fashion. This will make the kingdom secure from evil forever.[5]

Journey to the West is an excellent example of how Chinese mythology evolves from many different sources. Palmer and Xiaomin point out:

The story . . . illustrates more clearly than anything else the dynamic processes involved in Chinese mythology. For this is a culture where not only do historical individuals rise to become gods through imperial order, but characters from stories or novels are elevated by popular demand and belief.[6]

Glossary

alchemy—The process of mixing chemicals and potions that will transform something common into something special. Some of the goals of alchemy included changing base metals into gold, achieving immortality, and curing disease.

banquet—An elaborate meal that serves many dishes, usually held in honor of a special person or event.

Buddhism—A religion founded on the teachings of Siddhartha Gautama, also known as the Buddha. Among some beliefs are that greed causes suffering, meditation can help the individual achieve peace, and that living beings may be reborn into another life after they die.

calligraphy—The art of writing Chinese words on silk or paper, using a brush and ink.

Confucianism—A code of conduct developed by Confucius, a great teacher. This code emphasized obligations of people toward each other and toward their state.

demigod—A half-human, half-godlike ruler in early legendary Chinese mythology who could change shapes at will.

dynasty—A succession of rulers from the same family.

elixir—A magical potion that gives special powers to the person who drinks it.

I Ching—Translated as *The Book of Changes*, it is a book of philosophy as well as a tool for foretelling the future. It tells how to interpret trigrams, or patterns of lines, made by throwing down yarrow-plant sticks.

jade—A precious stone that is highly prized for its luster and hardness.

Journey to the West—One of the most popular Chinese novels about a journey to India to fetch the Buddhist scriptures and bring them back to China. This story involves a monkey, a pig, a monster, a horse, and a holy monk. They are guided on their way by Kuan Yin, the goddess of mercy.

li—A Chinese measurement equal to about one third of a mile.

octagon—An eight-sided figure.

phoenix—a mythical bird of peace, resembling a peacock.

pinyin—A system of converting Chinese words into English. This system is currently favored by Chinese scholars. The q is pronounced like "*ch,*" the x is pronounced like "*sh,*" and zh is pronounced like "*j.*"

pípa—A Chinese lute, or musical instrument.

quiver—A case for holding arrows.

sinologist—A scholar who studies the language and culture of the Chinese people.

Tao—Translated as "the Way," or a nature force.

Tao Te Ching—A collection of eighty-one verses written by the philosopher Lao-tzu, forming the basic ideas of Taoism.

Taoism—A religion based on the belief in the Tao, or the Way. It was originally a philosophy based on the 81 verses of the poet Lao-tzu.

trigram—A design made of three broken and/or solid lines. Each design stands for an important element—heaven, earth, fire, water, wind, storm, mountain, lake.

water spinach—A plant with thick hollow stems and long slender leaves. It needs very little water to grow.

yin-yang—Two opposing forces such as dark/light, weak/strong, winter/summer, death/life, female/male.

Chapter Notes

Preface

1. Martin Palmer and Zhao Xiaomin, *Essential Chinese Mythology* (San Francisco: HarperCollins, 1997), p. 2.
2. Brian P. Katz, *Deities and Demons of the Far East* (New York: Friedman/Fairfax Publishers, 1995), pp. 87–92.
3. Joseph Campbell, *The Masks of God: Oriental Mythology* (New York: Penguin Books, 1976), p. 378.

Chapter 1. Panku Creates the World

1. Joseph Campbell, *The Masks of God: Oriental Mythology* (New York: Penguin Books, 1976), p. 380.
2. Roy Willis, ed., *Mythology: An Illustrated Guide* (New York: Barnes and Noble, 1998), p. 19.
3. Martin Palmer and Zhao Xiaomin, *Essential Chinese Mythology* (San Francisco: HarperCollins, 1997), p. 12.

Chapter 2. Nuwa Creates People

1. Anne Birrell, *Chinese Mythology: An Introduction* (Baltimore, Md.: Johns Hopkins University Press, 1993), pp. 162–164.
2. Tao Tao Liu, "Chinese Myths and Legends" in *The Feminist Companion to Mythology*, Carolyne Larrington, ed. (London: HarperCollins, 1992), p. 230.
3. Jan and Yvonne Walls, *Classical Chinese Myths* (Hong Kong: Joint Publishing Co., Ltd., 1988), p. xi.
4. Birrell, p. 34.
5. Ibid.

Chapter 3. Fushi Teaches the People

1. Brian P. Katz, *Deities and Demons of the Far East* (New York: Friedman/Fairfax Publishers, 1995), pp. 87–92.
2. Derek Walters, *Chinese Mythology: An Encyclopedia of Myth and Legend* (London: The Aquarian Press, 1992), p. 67.
3. Chiang Yee, *The Chinese Eye: An Interpretation of Chinese Painting* (Bloomington: Indiana University Press, 1964), p. 17.

4. "Chinese Calligraphy," Encyclopedia Britannica, <http://www.britannica.com/bcom/eb/article/printable/0/0,5722,119420,00.html> (September 25, 2000).

5. Robert Shanmu Chen, *Asian Thought and Culture: A Comparative Study of Chinese and Western Cyclic Myths* (New York: Peter Lang Publishing, Inc., 1992), p. 51.

6. Ibid., p. 56.

Chapter 4. Water War

1. Anne Birrell, *Chinese Mythology: An Introduction* (Baltimore, Md.: Johns Hopkins University Press, 1993), pp. 97–98.

2. Derek Walters, *Chinese Mythology: An Encyclopedia of Myth and Legend* (London: The Aquarian Press, 1992), p. 41.

3. Carol Stepanchuck and Charles Wong, *Mooncakes and Hungry Ghosts: Festivals of China* (San Francisco: China Books and Periodicals, 1991), p. 49.

4. Anthony Christie, *Chinese Mythology* (Middlesex, England: Hamlyn Publishing Group Ltd., 1968), pp. 86–87.

5. Brian P. Katz, *Deities and Demons of the Far East* (New York: Friedman/Fairfax Publishers, 1995), p. 95.

6. Walters, p. 137.

7. T. C. Lai and Robert Mok, *Jade Flute: The Story of Chinese Music* (New York: Schocken Books, 1985), p. 23.

Chapter 5. Yu Rebuilds the Earth

1. Joseph Campbell, *The Masks of God: Oriental Mythology* (New York: Penguin Books, 1976), pp. 389–396.

2. Brian P. Katz, *Deities and Demons of the Far East* (New York: Friedman/Fairfax Publishers, 1995), p. 87.

3. Jan and Yvonne Walls, *Classical Chinese Myths* (Hong Kong: Joint Publishing Co., Ltd., 1988), p. ix.

4. Ibid., p. x.

5. John S. Major, *Heaven and Earth in Early Han Thought* (Albany: State University of New York Press, 1993), pp. 46–47.

Chapter 6. The Grand Archer Yi

1. E. T. C. Werner, *A Dictionary of Chinese Mythology* (Shanghai, China: Kelly and Walsh, Limited, 1932), p. 159.

2. Weed Science Society of America (WSSA), <http://ext. agn. uiuc.edu/wssa/subpages/weed/ws.htm> (April 19, 2000).

3. Sarah Allan, *The Shape of the Turtle: Myth, Art, and Cosmos in Early China* (Albany: State University of New York Press, 1991), p. 25.

4. Anne Birrell, *Chinese Mythology: An Introduction* (Baltimore, Md.: Johns Hopkins University Press, 1993), p. 78.

5. Anthony Christie, *Chinese Mythology* (Middlesex, England: Hamlyn Publishing Group Ltd., 1968), p. 60.

6. Birrell, p. 124.

7. Jan and Yvonne Walls, *Classical Chinese Myths* (Hong Kong: Joint Publishing Co., Ltd., 1988), p. 69.

8. "Handle This Spinach With Care" *Agricultural Research Service*, June 1998, <http://www.ars.usda.gov/is/AR/archive/ jun98/ spin0698.htm> (April 19, 2000).

9. Weed Science Society of America.

10. Ibid.

Chapter 7. The Moon Goddess

1. Koh Kok Kiang, *Legend of the Moon Maiden* (Singapore: Asiapac Books PTE LTD, 1996), p. i.

2. Roy Willis, ed., *Mythology: An Illustrated Guide* (New York: Barnes and Noble, 1998), p. 94.

3. Derek Walters, *An Encyclopedia of Myth and Legend* (London: Diamond Books, 1995), pp. 117–118.

4. Alexander Eliot, *The Universal Myths* (New York: Truman Talley Books/Meridian, 1976), p. 36.

5. Anne Birrell, *Chinese Mythology: An Introduction* (Baltimore, Md.: Johns Hopkins University Press, 1993), p. 173.

6. Tao Tao Liu. "Chinese Myths and Legends," in *The Feminist Companion to Mythology*, Carolyne Larrington, ed. (London: Pandora Press, HarperCollins, 1992), p. 234.

Chapter 8. The Unicorn's Prophecy

1. Liu Wu-Chi, *Confucius, His Life and Time* (New York: Philosophical Library, 1955), pp. 83–86.

2. William Edward Soothill, *The Analects of Confucius* (New York: Paragon Book Reprint Corp., 1968), p. 21.

3. Herrlee Glessner Creel, *Confucius: The Man and the Myth* (Westport, Conn.: Greenwood Press, 1972), p. 1.

4. René-Yvon Lefebvre d'Argencé, *Chinese Jades in the Avery Brundage Collection* (San Francisco: de Young Museum Society, 1972), p. 9.

5. Ibid.

6. Ibid.

Chapter 9. Monkey

1. Roy Willis, ed., *Mythology: An Illustrated Guide* (New York: Barnes and Noble, 1998), p. 98.

2. Fatima Wu, "Journey to the West" in *Great Literature of the Eastern World: The Major Works of Prose, Poetry and Drama from China, India, Japan, Korea and the Middle East*, Ian P. McGreal, ed. (New York: HarperCollins, 1996), p. 128.

3. Russell Kirkland, "The Book of the Way" in *Great Literature of the Eastern World: The Major Works of Prose, Poetry and Drama from China, India, Japan, Korea and the Middle East*, Ian P. McGreal, ed. (New York: HarperCollins, 1996), p. 24.

4. Witter Bynner, *The Chinese Translations: The Works of Witter Bynner, James Kraft,* ed. (New York: Farrar Straus and Giroux, 1978), pp. 335–336.

5. Kirkland, pp. 25–26.

Chapter 10. The Pilgrimage

1. Fatima Wu, "Journey to the West" in *Great Literature of the Eastern World: The Major Works of Prose, Poetry and Drama from China, India, Japan, Korea and the Middle East*, Ian P. McGreal, ed. (New York: HarperCollins, 1996), pp. 128–129.

2. Roy Willis, ed., *Mythology: An Illustrated Guide* (New York: Barnes and Noble, 1998), p. 96.

3. Daniel L. Overmyer, *Religions of China: the World as a Living System* (San Francisco: Harper & Row, 1986), p. 43.

4. Martin Palmer and Jay Ramsay with Man-Ho Kwok, *Kuan Yin: Myths and Prophecies of the Chinese Goddess of Compassion* (London: Thorsons, HarperCollins, 1995), p. xii.

5. Martin Palmer and Zhao Xiaomin, *Essential Chinese Mythology* (San Francisco: HarperCollins, 1997), p. 187.

6. Ibid., p. 37.

Further Reading

Giddens, Owen and Sandra. *Chinese Mythology (Mythology Around the World)*. New York: Rosen Central, 2006.

Shone, Rob. *Chinese Myths (Graphic Mythology)*. New York: Rosen Publishing Group, 2006.

Yang, Lihui and Anderson Turner, Jessica. *Handbook of Chinese Mythology*. New York: Oxford University Press, 2008.

Internet Addresses

Ancient Chinese Mythology
<http://www.crystalinks.com/chinamythology.html>

World Myths for Children
<http://www.archive.org/details/kzzs003>

Index